The SAP® Material Master— a Practical Guide, 2nd edition

Matthew Johnson

Thank you for purchasing this book from Espresso Tutorials!

Like a cup of espresso coffee, Espresso Tutorials SAP books are concise and effective. We know that your time is valuable and we deliver information in a succinct and straightforward manner. It only takes our readers a short amount of time to consume SAP concepts. Our books are well recognized in the industry for leveraging tutorial-style instruction and videos to show you step by step how to successfully work with SAP.

Check out our YouTube channel to watch our videos at *https://www.youtube.com/user/EspressoTutorials*.

If you are interested in SAP Finance and Controlling, join us at *http://www.fico-forum.com/forum2/* to get your SAP questions answered and contribute to discussions.

Related titles from Espresso Tutorials:

▶ Claudia Jost: First Steps in the SAP® Purchasing Processes (MM)
  http://5016.espresso-tutorials.com

▶ Björn Weber: First Steps in the SAP® Production Processes (PP)
  http://5027.espresso-tutorials.com

▶ Sydnie McConnell & Martin Munzel: First Steps in SAP® (2nd edition)
  http://5045.espresso-tutorials.com

▶ Stephen Birchall: Invoice Verification for SAP®
  http://5073.espresso-tutorials.com

▶ Kevin Riddell, Rajen Iyver: Practical Guide to SAP® GTS, Part 1: SPL Screening and Compliance Management
  http://5100.espresso-tutorials.com

▶ Avijt Dutta & Shreekant Shiralkar: Demand Planning with SAP® APO—Concepts and Design
  http://5105.espresso-tutorials.com

▶ Avijt Dutta & Shreekant Shiralkar: Demand Planning with SAP® APO—Execution
  http://5106.espresso-tutorials.com

▶ Kevin Riddell, Rajen Iyver: Practical Guide to SAP® GTS, Part 2: Preference and Customs Management
  http://5134.espresso-tutorials.com

▶ Tobias Götz, Anette Götz: Practical Guide to SAP® Transportation Management (2nd edition)
  http://5082.espresso-tutorials.com

Matthew Johnson
The SAP® Material Master — a practical Guide, 2nd edition

ISBN:	978-1-5463-0417-3
Editor:	Lisa Jackson
Cover Design:	Philip Esch, Martin Munzel
Cover Photo:	fotolia #109234498 (c) WilliamJu
Interior Design:	Johann-Christian Hanke

All rights reserved.

2nd Edition 2017, Gleichen

© 2017 by Espresso Tutorials GmbH

URL: *www.espresso-tutorials.com*

Feedback
We greatly appreciate any kind of feedback you have concerning this book. Please mail us at *info@espresso-tutorials.com*.

Table of Contents

Preface

Hello SAP Material Master users!

SAP Material Master can be a difficult section of SAP to interact with at first. It is comprised of many different parameter settings pertaining to a wide range of business functions, which are all related to managing the materials in your organization. It can take years of experience to understand how each business function relates to another within the software. With a little curiosity and motivation, your understanding of these relationships, as well as your understanding of SAP, will expand over time. It has been three years now since I've written the first edition of this book and my own skills and understanding have continued to mature. Because of this experience, I am happy to present a deeper look into SAP Material Master.

My intention has always been to offer a text for the beginner to novice-level end user of SAP Material Master in a multitude of manufacturing and distribution environments. The text is suited for MRP controllers, master schedulers, material buyers, material planners, inventory control and warehouse personnel, sales order management administrators, and the consultants and institutions who educate those individuals. The text contains standard how-to and why-do explanations of each field that you will encounter. It also offers case examples for a detailed explanation of the most useful components of the material master, as well as useful tips that are derived from my years of successful materials management. I'm taking this opportunity to include feedback from first-edition readers, as well as refinements and improved tactics I've learned over the past three years while in the materials management trade.

For those of you just starting out with material master, I recommend that you read the entire book to build a strong understanding of the material master framework in your mind. For those of you who are already immersed in the SAP Material Master environment, this text contains practical application examples that can be used as a reference when new ERP solutions are required in your organization.

Acknowledgements

As always, I would like to thank all of those in my family who supported me through the process of writing the first book and now the second edition. I would like to thank the leadership at Martin-Baker America, Inc. for their continued support. Finally, I would like to thank Espresso Tutorials for their commitment to producing exceptional SAP educational materials.

Good luck and enjoy,

Matt

We have added a few icons to highlight important information. These include:

Tips

Tips highlight information that provides more details about the subject being described and/or additional background information.

Examples

Examples help illustrate a topic better by relating it to real world scenarios.

Attention

Attention notices highlight information that you should be aware of when you go through the examples in this book on your own.

Finally, a note concerning the copyright: all screenshots printed in this book are the copyright of SAP SE. All rights are reserved by SAP SE. Copyright pertains to all SAP images in this publication. For the sake of simplicity, we do not mention this specifically underneath every screenshot.

1 Introduction

In this chapter, I would like to introduce myself to you and describe how I got started working with SAP. I'll also describe what you can expect from the following chapters in this text.

Hello. My name is Matt Johnson, and just like you, I am an SAP end user. Fourteen years ago I began a career in manufacturing in the aerospace defense industry as a stock room clerk. In this entry-level position, I wouldn't have said that my prospects for success were very high. As it turned out, my timing could not have been better because our company was about to embark on a new adventure—implementing SAP software.

Implementing any new software, particularly an all-encompassing ERP system, can be a great equalizer in an organization. Everyone—from the CEO to the stock room clerk—has to learn something entirely new. The new software will not only impact how we do business, it will also impact how we communicate with one another. Because of this, the best practice is to bring together a diverse cross section of administrative personnel and end users alike to form an implementation team. This diversity creates the opportunity for the team to view the ERP system from different functional perspectives and ensure that system practices are implemented in consideration of the average user's needs.

I was lucky enough to be included on the implementation team. Immediately, I could see that learning as much as I could about SAP software would be beneficial to both my responsibilities within the company and my personal career path. This bit of luck combined with hard work, formal education, proper mentoring, and an interest in being both a student and teacher has culminated in a sound understanding of materials management in SAP.

I won't pretend that it was easy. It has been a long road. Together with my fellow employees, we experienced many successes and failures in our attempts to understand SAP's inner workings. Those of us concerned with operations and inventory management focused on the MM and PP modules. We tried several different approaches to grasp the concepts. We learned from our superiors, who were trained in SAP first.

We hired consultants. We read books. We tried different scenarios and tested them in a development client. It was not one, but all of these approaches combined that helped us to develop our understanding of these modules.

As you will see, the material master is at the heart of SAP materials management. There are several texts available to instruct you on the many technical aspects of SAP materials management. I've read through some of them over the years and like many text books written about software, those books will not only bore you to tears, but they are also often written at such a complex technical level that only the finest programmers can understand them. Often this is because how-to books are written by developers rather than users, and while a developer's understanding may be comprehensive, their ability to convey to real-world practice is usually lacking. Over the years, I've often thought that it would be very helpful for those of us who use SAP every day to have a practical text to rely on. It should be a text that can convey the basic concepts of the material master's software logic, while also providing a means for instruction on the necessary tasks and preferences of the end user. This book has been written based on those ideas and I hope that the format that I chose will effectively convey these concepts and shorten your SAP Material Master learning curve. The SAP Material Master is an information set that drives many different business functions. Its input also comes from many diverse roles within an organization. Because of this, I believe that this book will be useful for many different users including MRP controllers, master schedulers, material buyers, material planners, inventory control and warehouse personnel, sales order management administrators, and the consultants and institutions who educate those individuals.

I have had the unique experience of acting in several different roles in my career, all of which have pertained to the material master. Therefore, I have written each section of this book from the perspective of the end user performing the relevant tasks. Each chapter will conclude with a personal experience that has helped me to grow in my knowledge of the material master and will hopefully help you to avoid some common mistakes. In the following chapters, we will cover:

- ▶ Material master basics—This chapter will discuss how to create and access the material master. It will also explain how to enter information, as well as how data is stored and retrieved. I will provide explanations of global versus plant-specific settings and instructions on how to access help and technical information.

▶ Manufacturing environment—In this chapter, I will explain the types of manufacturing environments (make-to-stock, make-to-order, repetitive, etc.) and how each applies to the material master. I will compare and contrast to differentiate each type and will guide the user in the decision.

▶ Basic information—In this chapter, we will begin to look at each of the fields within each screen of the material master and look at possible selections and their consequences, along with useful tips for cost saving measures where appropriate. This chapter will focus on basic information (unit of measure, descriptions, material groupings, revision control, etc.)

▶ Sales—In this chapter, I will discuss sales units and groups, tax data, pricing groups, additional sales classifications, tax data, foreign trade, etc. We'll also look at how the settings impact customers, other units in the organization, and other modules in SAP.

▶ Purchasing—This chapter will focus on the items that affect procurement such as purchasing groups, purchasing value keys, quota arrangements, JIT indicators, foreign trade, and purchase order text. I have included useful tips about cost effective procurement techniques.

▶ Planning—This is where the heart of production lies. It is also where organizations can implement the most cost-effective measures. I will provide several useful tips in regard to effective planning. I will also explain differences in MRP types. We'll cover reorder point planning in detail, and I will touch on its use in lean manufacturing environments. We'll discuss specific parameters and their consequences and benefits. A valuable bonus section has been added for the second edition which details a very useful technique called *subcontracting*.

▶ Inventory management—In this chapter, we will discuss cycle counting, shelf life, plant storage data, and the material picking process.

▶ Quality management—In this chapter, I will discuss the general inspection data setup and where it affects other areas within the organization.

▶ Accounting—This chapter will discuss standard price versus moving average price, cost estimates, LIFO and FIFO, overhead calculation, costed versus non-costed materials, profit centers, stock valuation, etc.

I would like to emphasize that managing the material master, along with most SAP functions, is a team effort. Input will be provided by end users from several different functional silos within your organization. I also recommend that you learn to trust and openly communicate with one another as much as possible. You will learn a great deal about your own role in the material master by also learning how it relates to the roles of others. After all, the most effective team is one that can manage its diversity in a productive manner in order to use all skill sets harmoniously. Good luck and enjoy.

2 Material master basics

In this chapter, I will describe the general format of the SAP Material Master as it is seen by the end user. I will also set up a framework for my description of the material master by defining some terms that will be used throughout the text. This framework will help you begin navigating the material master.

By maintaining a material master, you will not only be describing an item, you will also be further classifying that item to suit your organization's needs.

You will set up the material master to perform various sales, planning, procurement, production, and shipping activities, as well as selecting the parameters to control those actions. As we go through this text, I will define the material master settings and their implications in detail. In order to do this, we need to discuss the basic theory and abilities of the material master, as well as define some common terms that will be used throughout the text.

2.1 Material master structure

Like most information stored within SAP's transactions, the material master is nothing more than a database that has been programmed with an aesthetic visual representation. This visually pleasing display consists of several *screens*, each containing information and parameter settings relevant to the screen's title. Furthermore, the information on each screen is sub-classified into more specific groupings, which I'll refer to as an *information set*. The example below (see Figure 2.1) is a picture of the MRP 1 screen, an essential component to material planning, procurement, and production functionality. This screen consists of some general header data: the material, the material description, technical information, the plant and the revision. It also consists of four information sets: GENERAL DATA, MRP PROCEDURE, LOT SIZE DATA, and MRP AREAS.

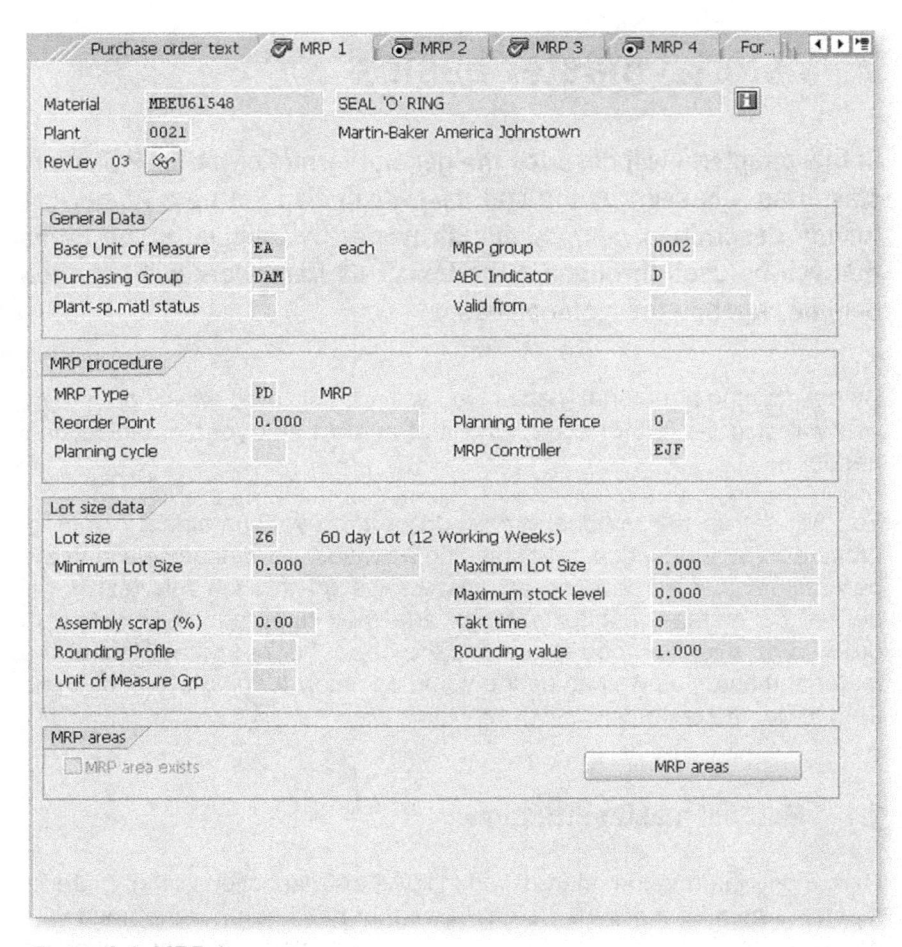

Figure 2.1: MRP 1 screen

Each element of any given information set is called a *field*. In the previous example (see Figure 2.1), the information set GENERAL DATA contains the fields BASE UNIT OF MEASURE, MRP GROUP, PURCHASING GROUP, ABC INDICATOR, PLANT SPECIFIC MATERIAL STATUS, and VALID FROM (regarding plant-specific material status).

Each field is also stored "behind the scenes" in a *table* within the SAP database. The table contains other fields with similar functions. SAP has also designed relationship structures into the program which allow certain tables to communicate with one another and drive functionality. As you progress in your understanding of the material master, you will want to understand those relationships in great detail. Not only will an understanding of those relationships help you to understand material master functionality, it will also help you to capitalize on customized reporting possibilities.

Each table and field is represented by a technical name in the database. In the example below (see Figure 2.2) a technical description of the field MRP TYPE is displayed. Here you can see the technical name of the field (DISMM) and the table (MARC) in which it is stored. We will discuss more about technical information and how to access it later in the chapter.

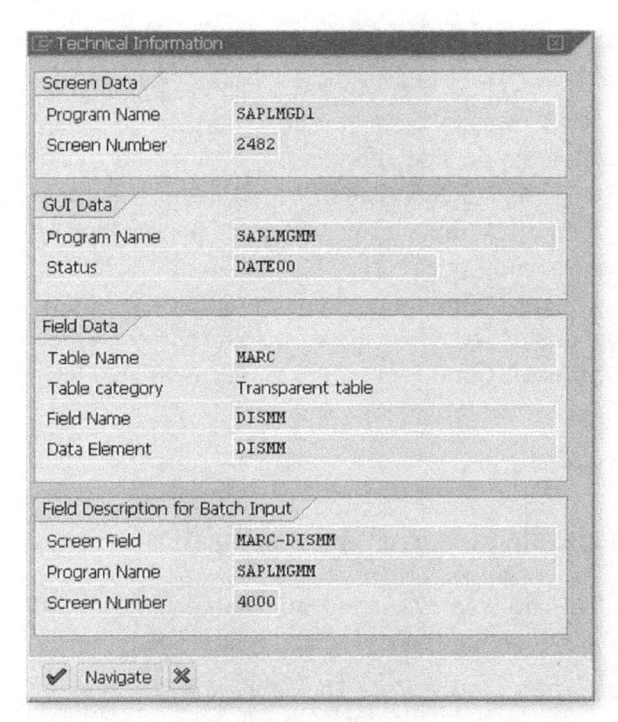

Figure 2.2: Technical information—table and field name

Use table relationships for customized reporting

 Not all of the information you may want is available to you in a standard SAP report. Once you've gained an understanding of tables, fields, and their relationships with one another in the material master, explore transaction SQVI. It is a report builder where you can create customized reports on most interrelated fields of the material master (and other transactions for that matter) by joining their respective tables for the purposes of reporting.

Advanced tip: Use SQ01, SQ02, and SQ03 to share joined table reports

 Transaction SQVI is a quick and handy tool for the individual end user to join tables in order to generate simple reports. I recommend SQVI to the beginner because of its simplicity. However, once you become confident with joining tables for ad hoc reporting I recommend using transactions SQ01, SQ02, and SQ03. These transactions allow the user to define information sets (table or collection of joined tables) and allow for more refinements to the selection criteria and output. Furthermore, an end user can define authorized user groups for these information sets so that customized reports can be shared and reproduced by any authorized user. SQVI limits the use of the defined table join to only the end user who created it.

2.2 Creating and accessing the SAP Material Master

There are three main SAP transaction codes that pertain to the SAP Material Master:

> ▶ MM01 (CREATE MATERIAL MASTER)—This is the transaction code used to create a new material master. You will have two choices when you create a material master. You can either create a new material without reference, or you can choose to copy an exist-

ing material master and then change the relevant settings to account for the new material.

▶ MM02 (CHANGE MATERIAL MASTER)—This transaction code allows you to make changes to existing material masters. However, not all elements of a material master can be amended in this transaction. For instance, the industry sector and material type are fixed once a material master is created. The material type can be changed, but through a separate transaction and certain restrictions apply.

▶ MM03 (DISPLAY MATERIAL MASTER)—This transaction code simply allows you to display a given material master. By design, no changes may take place in this transaction.

2.2.1 Creating the material master

To create a material master, you will enter transaction code MM01. Once you've done that, you will be presented with the following screen containing five fields (see Figure 2.3).

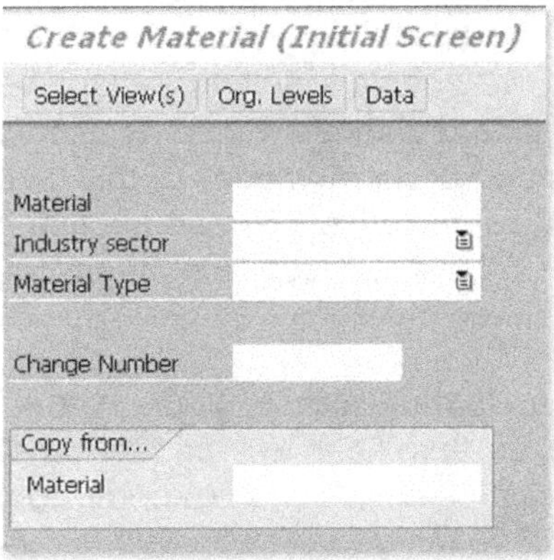

Figure 2.3: Create material—opening screen

MATERIAL—In this field you will enter the alphanumeric material number you wish to create. There are two schools of thought in the numbering scheme, you can either leave this field blank and SAP will automatically assign the next available number, or you can enter a number of your choosing. Either way, the numbering scheme and range of numbers must be defined in SAP customizing. The number can consist of up to 18 alphanumeric characters.

Use your own numbering scheme

 I recommend that your company develop its own numbering scheme containing both letters and numbers for three reasons. First, this practice helps to organize products and product families. Second, by maintaining your own numbering system, you will be far less likely to confuse your parts with customer or supplier part numbers if those entities maintain similar components. Finally, employees are more likely to recognize materials and their respective numbers from memory if a logical descriptive numbering scheme is used, saving valuable look-up time when they need to identify a component.

INDUSTRY SECTOR—In this field, you will classify the segment of industry for which your part is being created. In most cases, an organization will use only one industry sector. By making this choice, you are defining the sequence of the available screens and the available fields within those screens. Once you create the material master, this setting cannot be changed. SAP will come with several standard choices. However, others are easily added through SAP customizing. For the purposes of this text, we will assume a general industry setting based on a manufacturing environment. The other standard choices will include the chemical, pharmaceuticals, engineering, and retail industries.

MATERIAL TYPE—This field allows you to further classify your material master application. The entries made in this field will control what screens will exist for the material and what fields will require entry from the user. You can assign different material number ranges to each material type for further refinement.

Case example: Non-valuated materials

John wishes to control the procurement and inventory quantity of his shop floor aides such as rags and working gloves. However, he does not want the expense of those items to be included in the cost of goods sold, nor does he wish to maintain cost estimates or accounting data for those items. John decides to create material numbers for his shop floor aides with the material type 'Non-valuated materials.' This material type does not use the Costing or Accounting screens. He now has the ability to purchase shop floor aides by using SAP's reorder point planning logic without the need to maintain costing and accounting views. He also has the added benefit of using a material number range specific to shop floor aides that will help to identify their use within the plant. You might ask yourself, how will the expense be accounted for in the balance sheet if there is no standard cost assigned to the item? The answer is simple. When one places a requisition for a non-valuated material, SAP automatically prompts you to make a mandatory account assignment to a cost center and general ledger account. The price of the material entered into the purchase order is then assigned to your specified account.

Change number—Think of this as revision control to your material master, although it is not the same as the revision control of the material's engineering drawing. This field can be used to track changes made to the material master itself. You can choose not to use this feature, as changes you make to the material master are still recorded and can be reported. However, by maintaining a change number you can control things like serial number usage by assigning valid dates to the change number. Furthermore, this feature will allow you to control the release of changes to certain areas within the company.

Copy from—By entering an existing material number in this field, the fields of the new material master you are creating will default to the values of the material master you are copying. This can be a quick way to create a material master that has similar characteristics to an existing one. However, you must use extreme caution. It is not likely that you will want every field entry in the new material master to be identical to the existing one. Fortunately, when you are copying a material master for the creation of a new one, you will be presented with each screen to review as you are performing the copy.

Once you have entered your necessary data into the fields we've just discussed, you will then need to select the specific views (screens) that you wish to create for the material. This can be done by clicking on the SELECT VIEW(S) icon (see Figure 2.3). You will then be presented with the SELECT VIEW(S) screen (see Figure 2.4). Here you will highlight your desired screens by clicking on the SELECT icon to the left of each view. Be sure to select the CREATE VIEWS SELECTED indicator at the bottom of the screen. Once you are happy with your choices, press ⌐Enter⌐ or click on the green checkmark.

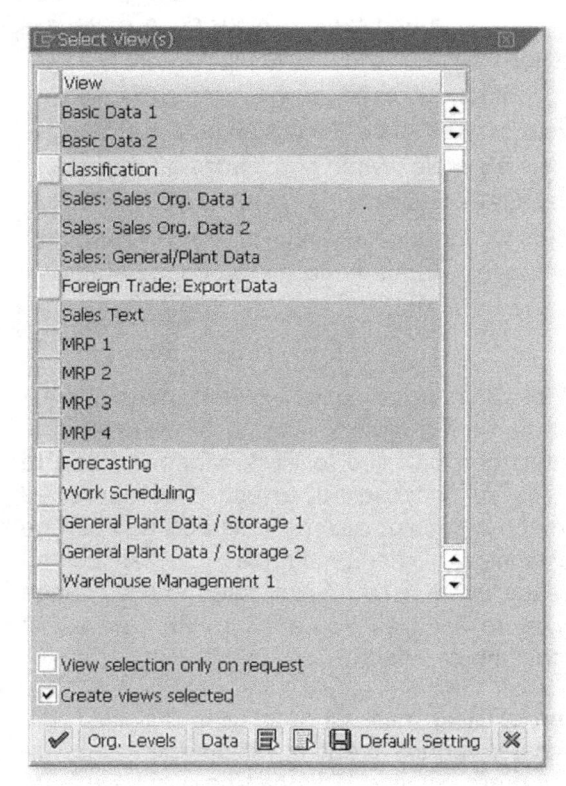

Figure 2.4: Select View(s) screen

Once you've completed your selections in the SELECT VIEW(S) screen and pressed ⌈Enter⌉, you will be presented with the final preliminary entry screen before you enter the material master. That screen is the ORGANIZATIONAL LEVELS screen (see Figure 2.5).

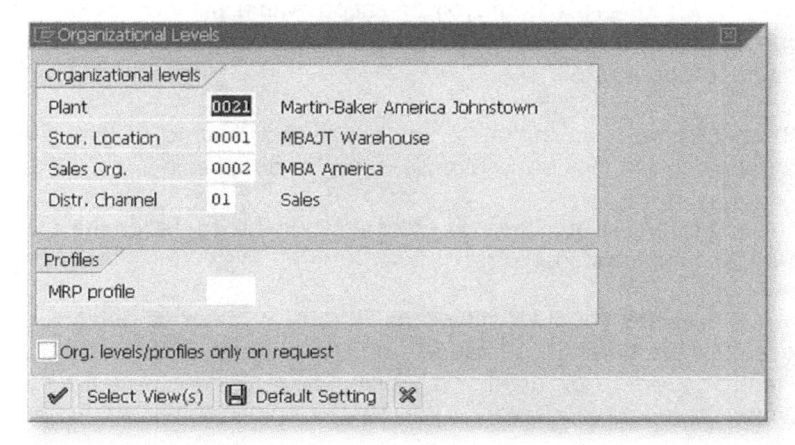

Figure 2.5: Organizational Levels screen

In this screen, you must define the PLANT, storage location (STOR. LOCATION), sales organization (SALES ORG.), distribution channel (DISTR. CHANNEL), and other required profiles of the material master. If you are copying from an existing material, you will also need to define those values from which the new material master is to be copied (see Figure 2.6). In this example, more customized controls exist, as the warehouse and distribution are complex. You may or may not have these features depending on your environment.

PLANT—This field is simply the plant for which you are creating the material master. A material master must be created for each plant in which you wish to maintain the material. Some fields in the material master will be *global*, and other settings in the material master will be *plant-specific*. Global settings are those settings that will apply to a given material in all plants within your organization. So if you enter a setting into a global field, it will be the same setting for all plants. Conversely, if you enter a setting into a plant-specific field, that setting only applies to the plant you are creating or changing. As we progress through the book, I will define each field as either global or plant-specific.

STORAGE LOCATION—This is the number of the storage location where the material will be kept. You can have multiple storage locations within one plant. This feature is very useful in plants with multiple buildings.

SALES ORGANIZATION—This is the organization within the company responsible for the sale of certain products. This field is useful for segregating major product lines.

DISTRIBUTION CHANNEL—In this field, you define the method of distribution. The main choices include wholesale, retail, or direct sales.

WAREHOUSE NUMBER—Here you will enter the number representing the physical warehouse for storage.

STORAGE TYPE—Here you can select the type of storage to guide the goods receipt of the item. For instance, you can choose 'High rack storage' for items that are rarely used and 'Picking area' for items that are for everyday use.

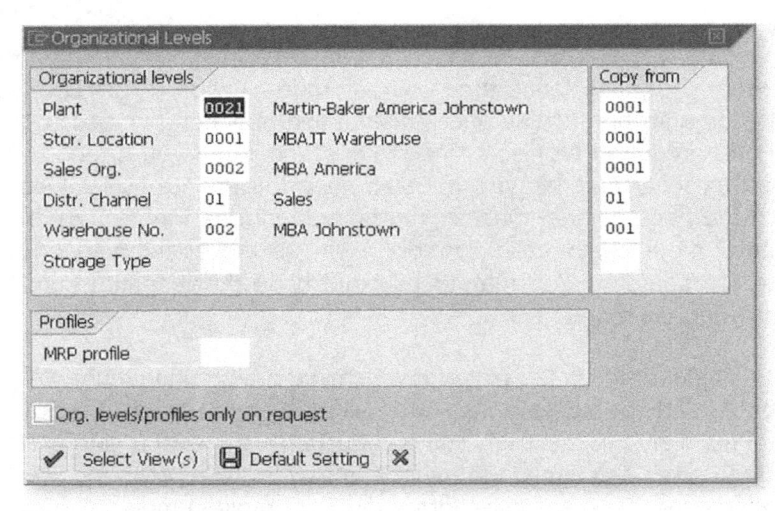

Figure 2.6: Organizational Levels—copy mode screen

Storage locations and types can have limited access

You can define rules in SAP customizing that block the issue or receipt of goods in any given storage location or type to prevent unwanted inventory movements. In my organization, we use a particular storage location to store items to be sold specifically as spare parts. These same items are also used in general production. To stop ourselves from inadvertently consuming the items designated for spare part sales, we transfer them to a location that does not allow automatic goods issue to production orders.

2.2.2   Accessing the material master

Generally, authorizations to create and change a material master are only granted to the appropriate individuals within an organization to provide a means of control and reduce the risk of erroneous entries. After all, choices made in the material master have far reaching consequences. If someone were to inadvertently make a change to a given material master, there could be serious consequences resulting in lost profits. However, everyone should be authorized to display or view the material master for informational purposes. For that reason, the display of the material master can be reached through many different SAP screens. You can access the material master through either the MM03 DISPLAY MATERIAL MASTER transaction code or the MM02 CHANGE MATERIAL MASTER transaction code, but one can also arrive at the material master in display mode by double clicking on the material number in any SAP screen where the material number is underlined. In the following example of the STOCK REQUIREMENTS LIST screen (see Figure 2.7) you will find that the material number is underlined. By double clicking on the material number, you will be taken to the material master display mode.

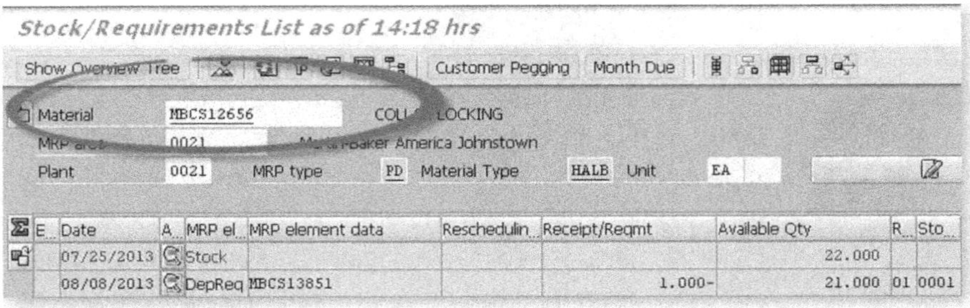

Figure 2.7: Stock/Requirements List—underlined material number

You will find that the STOCK REQUIREMENTS LIST screen is a natural partner to the material master. In this screen, you can see the current status of the material's inventory and both planned and actual requirements and supply. I often find myself going back and forth between the STOCK REQUIREMENTS LIST screen and its related material master to see why materials are being planned the way they are. The double-click feature is a nice way to bounce back and forth between the two. You should expect to become very familiar with the STOCK REQUIREMENTS LIST screen (see Figure 2.8), SAP transaction code MD04, as it will be a constant reference for all of your MRP activities.

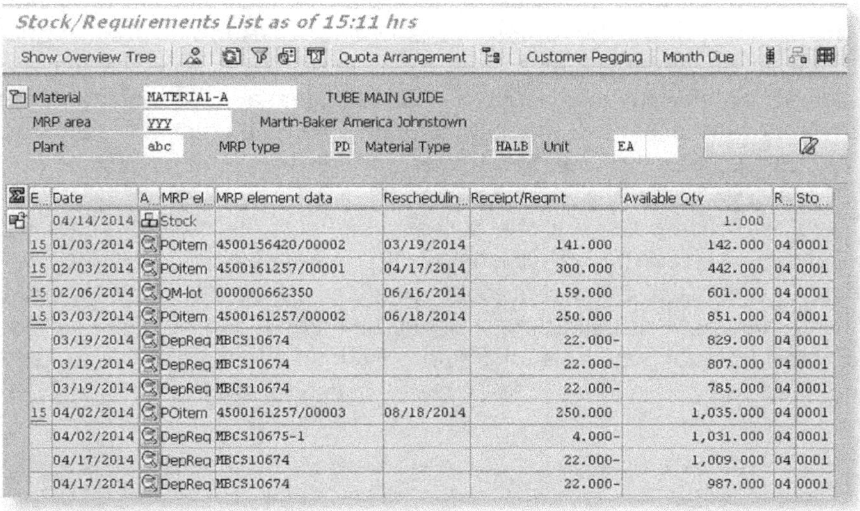

Figure 2.8: Stock/Requirements List screen

However, because this screen shows every element of supply and demand generated by MRP, the list can be quite cumbersome and go on for many pages. As a buyer, particularly in a larger organization, you may not be interested in filing through the many elements of demand that are causing requisitions to be generated. It may be more efficient for you to view only the information that concerns you. This refinement is readily available to you in the opening screen of the STOCK/REQUIREMENTS LIST transaction, known as a filter (see Figure 2.9).

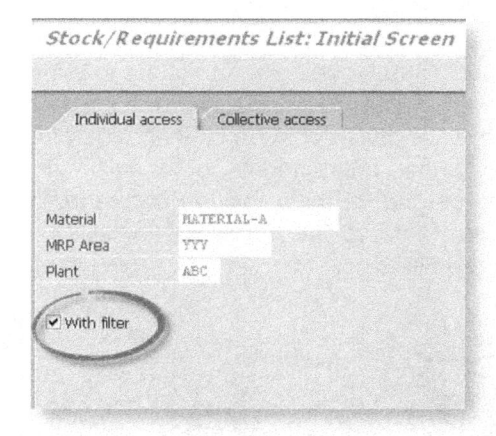

Figure 2.9: With filter field checked

By setting the WITH FILTER field to active, you will have the ability to filter your display to the following selections:

- ▶ All in replenishment lead time
- ▶ All in 10 days
- ▶ Display horizon for the user
- ▶ All process proposals to the vendor
- ▶ Firm process proposals to the vendor
- ▶ Fixed process proposals to the vendor
- ▶ Only make-to-order planning
- ▶ Only receipts
- ▶ Only requirements and stock
- ▶ Requirements and firmed receipts
- ▶ Display all

You can further refine your output by using the selection rule. In this field, you have the following refinement choices:

- ▶ Delivery schedule instead of schedule lines
- ▶ Only receipts
- ▶ Planned independent requirements with dependent requirements
- ▶ Requirements and stocks
- ▶ Without planned independent requirements

In the screen below, (see Figure 2.10), I have selected the filters to show receipts only. This is very useful for a buyer who is interested in tracking his or her current purchase orders, as well as getting a look at upcoming plans for purchase orders, without being distracted by other MRP elements. Furthermore, any filter you set can be held for you permanently by going to SETTINGS once you have entered the STOCK/REQUIREMENTS LIST screen and selecting the desired filters.

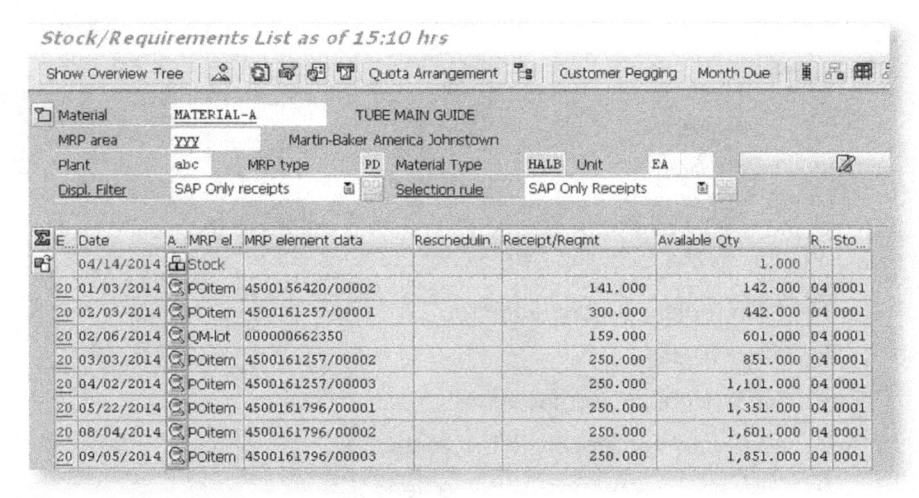

Figure 2.10: With filter—receipts only

2.3 Accessing technical help and information

The SAP help function is one of the most useful help tools I've ever encountered in a software application. There are several forms of help available and each method will allow you to reach a different level of technical assistance. In many cases, you will be provided with technical information that points you towards the section of SAP customizing where your concern can be addressed. In others, you will be provided with the necessary technical information, such as table and field name, to allow you to understand the existing relationship between a field and another entity. By accessing any one or combination of the available help avenues, you will most likely find a solution to your problem. In any event, you are sure to gain a better perspective on your inquiry which will assist in communicating with SAP about the issue at hand. I recommend referring to SAP help as often as you can. This activity can greatly increase your understanding of SAP logic.

2.3.1 General SAP help and information

Access to the standard SAP help menu can be found on every SAP screen by selecting HELP in the uppermost tool bar. As you can see in the following example (see Figure 2.11), there are several forms of standard help. Each selection will assist you in a different way.

▶ APPLICATION HELP—This selection will direct you to help about the current transaction you are viewing.

▶ SAP LIBRARY—This selection will show you information on all of SAP's offerings for various industries.

▶ GLOSSARY—Here you can find an index of all SAP terms.

▶ RELEASE NOTES—A release note is an addition or change to the software that occurs between full system revision releases. By clicking here, you can search for information on active release notes.

▶ SAP SERVICE MARKETPLACE—This is a direct link to the SAP services website. Here, you can find links to contact SAP directly for technical assistance.

▶ CREATE SUPPORT MESSAGE—If this feature is configured, you can create a message to send to your support staff.

▶ SETTINGS—Here you can define how system help messages are displayed within SAP.

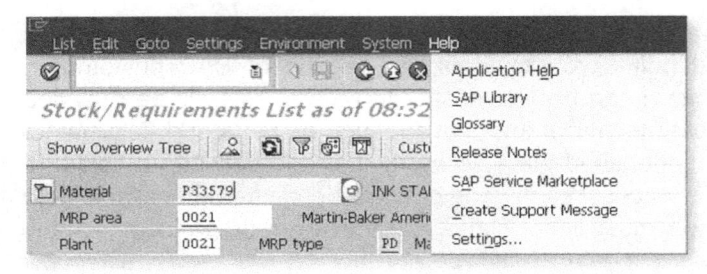

Figure 2.11: SAP Help

2.3.2 Performance assistant and technical information

While the SAP help features listed in the toolbar are valuable, nothing will assist your material master knowledge base more than accessing the performance assistant. This activity allows you to get specific information on any field that you are interested in. This information will include a definition of the field, the specific use of the field, and many times an example of the field's application. In the following example, you will see the performance assistance for the field PLANT-SPECIFIC MATERIAL STATUS, which you can find in the MRP 1 screen of the material master (see Figure 2.12). This information can be found for any field by placing your cursor in the desired field and pressing F1 on your keyboard.

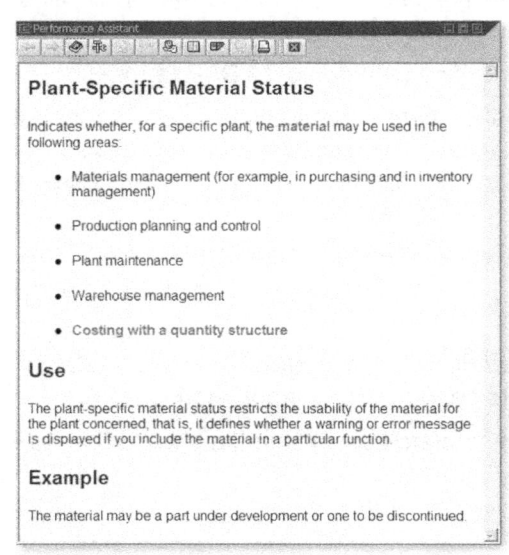

Figure 2.12: Performance Assistant screen

Another great benefit of the performance assistance is access to the field's technical information as described in section 2.1 (see Figure 2.2). By clicking on the TECHNICAL INFORMATION icon (see Figure 2.13), you will find information on the desired field in regard to its table structure and data storage.

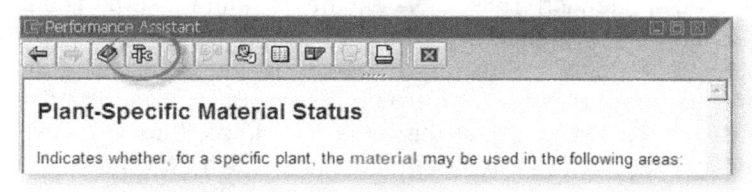

Figure 2.13: Technical information icon

2.4 Personal experience

At one point in my career, I became a production planning supervisor for a manufacturing facility. A significant function of this role was to create and maintain all material masters for the plant. While it was a wonderful learning experience and probably helped to increase my understanding of the material master more than any other assignment, it was also a tedious and time-consuming effort.

By this point in time, I had a solid understanding of the basic functions of the material master. I could create and maintain material masters to suit the facility's requirements. However, when a new product came along, I was forced to spend several days creating material masters in accordance with the new bill of material structure and analyzing each field entry to ensure that it was appropriate for each material. While this activity is far from entertaining, it is not the time for one to lose motivation. After all, the material masters and the settings that you are creating within them are going to be the foundation for most organizational activities.

After several rounds of new product implementations, I began to run out of steam. I needed to find a way to streamline the material master creation process, and due to the nature of material masters, mass creation is not a possibility. What I found through repetition is that most of the settings I was making in each material master were identical throughout each item within the BOM structure. They contained the same material groups, the same purchasing groups, the same MRP settings, and the list goes on. The differences from one material master to the next only involved about 10 fields.

After I recognized the pattern, I had a solution to my streamlining problem. I could develop a list of screens that contained fields that required changes or special attention. I also detailed the list with those particular fields so I would only pay attention to the necessary fields. That way I could create one material master from scratch for the particular BOM structure and use it as a basis for creating others. By copying the first material master I created to create the remaining items, I could quickly pass through the unchanging screens and focus strictly on those that needed special attention.

I won't say that this is extremely simple or without risk. You must understand the material master settings and their consequences in great detail before assuming the risk of copying them. With time and experience, you will develop this confidence. This little trick saved me a few days of agonizing data entry once I got into the rhythm.

An alternative to this method when creating several very similar material masters is to allow them to be created with identical entries in every field when performing the copy from one material master to the next. Once they've been saved, you can use SAP transaction MM17 to update just the unique fields for all materials in one effort.

In the example below (see Figure 2.14), I've created five very similar material masters that simply require different rounding values. In this screen, you can quickly make the necessary changes to all five material masters at once by entering your material numbers and plant in the opening screen and then typing each desired entry into the field you are updating (in this case it's ROUNDING VALUE) To complete the update, click on the save icon 🖫.

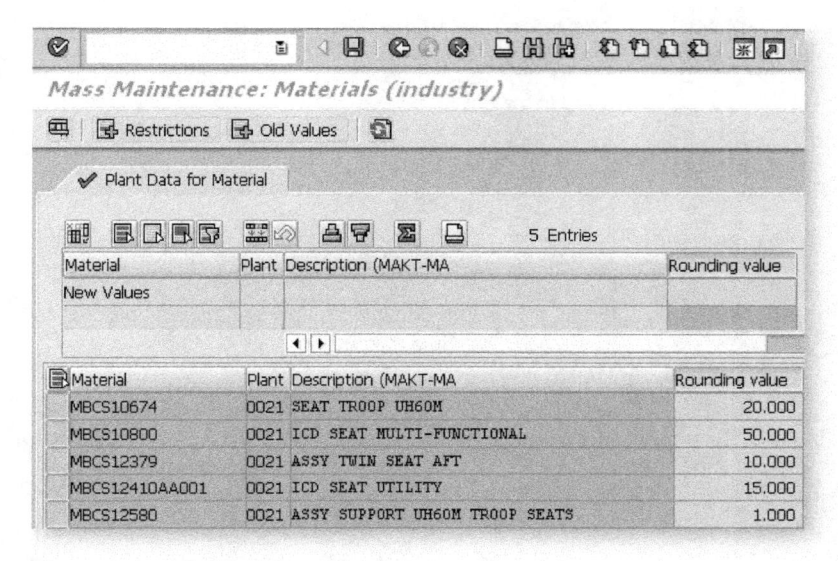

Figure 2.14: MM17—Mass Maintenance: Materials screen

3 Manufacturing environment

In this chapter, I will discuss the standard types of manufacturing environments and how their respective planning strategies are incorporated into SAP.

The setup and customizing of your material master will largely depend upon the manufacturing environment in which you are engaged. This manufacturing environment is shaped by several factors such as your product family and type, customer demand rate, product lifecycle, organizational structure, and corporate strategy.

When an organization is defining its corporate objectives, its governing body will take into consideration the factors listed above. The people at the top must consider the type of product they are making. Will the sales volume require a large amount of inventory? Will the product's lifecycle last very long? Does the company have the capacity to meet the projected demand? The officers of the company must decide the level of work to be completed at their manufacturing facility and which activities to outsource. This is usually based upon the company's core competencies and the amount of workforce they wish to employ.

Corporate leaders must also decide the level to which inventory should be maintained. Companies producing large volumes of homogeneous products will tend to keep a large inventory, while those who produce small batches of custom-made goods will keep very little finished product in stock. The decision makers must also consider customer satisfaction. Do they need the ability to deliver immediately? Will a large distribution network be utilized?

The answer to these questions might seem straightforward to you depending on your business. However, those answers must also be specifically defined in your material master in order to run your production strategy as planned. One of the very first choices your company will make in regard to the material master is defining your manufacturing strategy. In the following chapter, we'll discuss different types of manufacturing environments. While most of the steps discussed in this chapter are not managed within the material master, it is necessary for you to understand how SAP approaches planning strategies so that you can align the material master to your organizational needs.

3.1 Planning strategy in theory

In the manufacturing world, there are many different combinations of planning strategies that can be tailored to fit an organization's corporate objectives. However, every company's planning strategy will be based on at least one of four main concepts: make-to-stock, assemble-to-order, make-to-order, and engineer-to-order. You may find that your company has a different strategy for each product family or that a hybrid of two or more strategies is used plant-wide. The strategy that your organization chooses is based upon the point in which the manufacturing process begins after the company receives the customer order. Some refer to this as the customer decoupling point. A basic description for each is shown below.

- ▶ Make-to-stock—In this environment, you are making finished goods and stocking them on the shelf to await a customer order. The design of the product is frozen and cannot be adjusted to the customer's requirements. This method will guarantee the shortest possible lead time to the customer. This strategy is typically used for products that have a high sales volume and little to no customizing. Normally with this method, a production schedule is generated from a sales forecast. Obviously, this strategy involves a certain amount of financial risk because forecasts will never be 100% accurate. Therefore, you may be left with unsold stock after the season or product lifecycle has ended.

- ▶ Assemble-to-stock—In this production strategy, a company maintains inventory of raw material and subcomponents of the finished product. When a customer order is received, those raw materials and subcomponents are made into finished goods for the specific customer order. This strategy generally involves stocking subcomponents from a production schedule that is based on a sales forecast. Semi-finished items are made into finished goods once a customer order has been received. This method will allow for limited customizing to the final product during final assembly according to the product variables allowed by the manufacturer's design. This strategy does come with a slightly longer lead time than make-to-stock. However, the financial risk will be reduced because the cost of final assembly labor will not be incurred until a firm customer order is received.

▶ Make-to-order—In this production environment, a company may or may not maintain inventory of raw material, but no further procurement or production will begin until a customer order is received. This method allows for more flexibility in customizing because no subcomponents are premade. However, customers still choose products from a list of the customized choices offered for any given design. It also goes without saying that the lead time for finished products in this environment will be longer than those in make-to-stock and assemble-to-stock environments. Forecasts are not generally used in this environment because procurement and production times are built into the overall lead time quoted to the customer. Therefore, actual customer orders will dictate the activities within MRP. Due to the nature of the customer order acceptance, the financial risk is very low.

▶ Engineer-to-order—This strategy will have the longest lead time of all, but it will also allow for the greatest amount of customizing and flexibility in design. With this method, a customer will provide the required amount of information to make the product to their specifications along with their order for that product. The manufacturer will then translate those specifications into a design and begin procurement and production. Again, forecasting is generally not used, as actual customer orders will drive MRP requirements. The financial risk here can vary. The risk may be low because procurement and production activities will not begin until an order is received. However, there may be significant risk in properly interpreting the customer's specifications.

As you will see in Figure 3.1, each production environment has its benefits, consequences, and risks. This matrix is a quick view for comparison.

Production Environment	Decoupling Point	Design Flexibility	Lead Time	Customization flexibility	MRP Activity	Financial Risk
Make-to-stock	shipped from inventory	none	hours to a few days	low	forecast	high
Assemble-to-stock	at sub component level	none	hours to a few days	low/medium	forecast/customer order	medium
Make-to-order	at raw component level	low	a few days to months	medium	customer order	low
Engineer-to-order	at design level	high	a few weekss to years	high	customer order	low/medium

Figure 3.1: Production environment matrix

3.2 SAP planning strategy

Now that you have an understanding of the different types of production environments, you can identify which one most closely resembles your organization. Remember, not every organization's planning strategy will fit simply into one category. You may be running a hybrid of two different strategies for any given material. Also, planning strategies may differ from material to material. In this section, I'll discuss the basic theory behind SAP planning strategies. Later, in Chapter 7, we'll discuss the field selections necessary to set up your planning strategy.

3.2.1 Strategy group

In the MRP 3 screen of the material master, you will select your planning strategy in the STRATEGY GROUP field (see Figure 3.2). There are several standard SAP strategies made available to you to fit most combinations of the theoretical planning strategies that we discussed in the section above (see section 3.1). If you are truly in a unique environment, you can create a customized strategy in SAP, but for most environments customizing is not necessary.

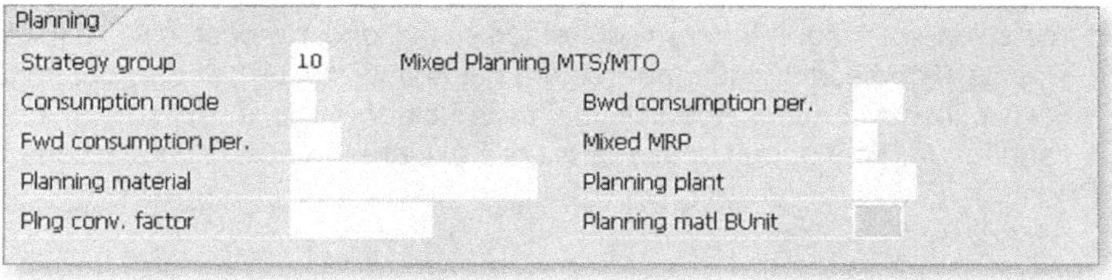

Planning			
Strategy group	10	Mixed Planning MTS/MTO	
Consumption mode		Bwd consumption per.	
Fwd consumption per.		Mixed MRP	
Planning material		Planning plant	
Plng conv. factor		Planning matl BUnit	

Figure 3.2: Planning—strategy group

Each strategy group determines how requirements are consumed and how stock availability is checked. The strategy group is made up of a combination of two different requirements types—independent requirements and customer requirements. The strategy group that you select will govern how MRP handles each type of requirement.

- ▶ Requirements type for independent requirements—These requirements are generated from a forecast for a given material. That forecast might stem from your sales and operations planning in the PP module, or it may simply be an independent requirement that you enter for a material to generate demand that would otherwise not exist (i.e. no customer order has been placed).

- ▶ Requirements type for customer requirements—These are requirements that are generated and dependent upon a customer order.

3.2.2 Defining the strategy group

The requirements types are linked to each strategy group, defined and fine-tuned in demand management customizing. As an end user, you will not be making the choices in the following fields, but it is important that you know how your materials are going to be treated by MRP. Below, I have included an example of a make-to-order strategy group as shown in customizing (see Figure 3.3). As you can see, what may seem like a simple choice in the strategy group field of the material master has far reaching consequences and controls many aspects of MRP. The PLANNING STRATEGY CUSTOMIZING screen consists of two main information

41

sets, one for independent requirements and one for customer requirements. The second customer requirements information set also contains two subsets, one to address the assemble-to-order environment, and another for configurable materials. Let's explore the possible selections.

Display View "Strategy": Details

Strategy	20 Make-to-order production

Requirements type of independent requirements

Reqmts type for indep.reqmts	
Reqmts class	
Consumption	
Planning Ind.	

Requirements type of customer requirements

Reqmt type of customer reqmt	KE	Indiv.cust.ord. w/o consumpt.
Requirements class	040	MkToOrdNoValW/o cons
Allocation indicat.		
No MRP	Requirement planned	☑ Availability check
Acct Assgt Cat.	E	☑ Requirement transfer
Settlement profile	SD1	☐ Req. Reduct.
Results analysis key	000004	

Assembly order

Assembly type	0 No assembly order processing	Online assembly	
Order Type		Capacity Check	
		☐ Component availability	

Configuration

Configuration	
Config. Consumption	

Figure 3.3: Planning strategy—make-to-order

Case example: Strategy group

 The Premium Hotel Goods Company (PHGC) produces a vast array of toiletry items that they sell to a wide variety of hotel classes around the globe. They have traditionally produced their non-customized goods in a make-to-stock environment according to a seasonal forecast. These items are offered commercially to any willing customer. Therefore, the requirements and financial settlement for all production and sales are homogeneous and only one strategy group has been maintained for all materials. Suddenly, the company is approached by a hotel mogul who is interested in offering custom-made towel and robe sets to match each hotel chain in his family of hotels. This will result in a 20% increase in overall sales for the PHGC. During negotiations, the company offers the hotel mogul special pricing for the large amount of business. This presents PHGC with a new problem. They must simultaneously run a production line of standard goods, made to a seasonal forecast, while also making custom goods for a customer with special pricing considerations. Furthermore, PHGC wants to settle the costs of the new production to a different account for analysis purposes. To prepare for this, PHGC creates a second strategy group for the new product line and inputs it into all material masters within that new product family. It will employ an assemble-to-order strategy with a separate settlement profile and results analysis key, allowing the separation of cost settlement between the two processes and furthermore separate profitability analysis. PHGC can now apply custom monograms to their towels with each order from the new hotel group upon the receipt of each order and still maintain their bulk production line in the make-to-stock environment.

Requirements type of independent requirements

In this information set, you will specifically define how independent requirements are handled within the selected strategy.

REQUIREMENTS TYPE FOR INDEPENDENT REQUIREMENTS—In this field, your customizer will select the requirements type for your strategy group relevant to independent entries in MRP. The requirements type will determine how independent requirements are consumed and the type of planning that will take place on a given material. Notice that in the example above (see Figure 3.3), no entry is made. That is because the planning strategy is make-to-order. In this example, it is a strict make-to-order environment. Therefore, no independent requirements should be considered. Had a make-to-stock planning strategy been selected, a requirements type to manage the MRP forecast would be present.

REQUIREMENTS CLASS—The requirements class dictates how material costing and financial settlement is to be carried out for the requirements type that has been chosen. This too is defined in customizing and once it is maintained, a requirements class will be automatically assigned to the appropriate requirements type.

CONSUMPTION—In a forecasted or make-to-order environment, you will normally wish to have your planned independent requirements reduced as actual customer orders are entered. This field will govern if and how independent requirements are consumed once a customer order is recognized in MRP. The entry made in this field is determined by your requirements type.

You will have four basic choices:

- ▶ No consumption with customer requirements—This is used for a make-to-stock strategy, where independent requirements are only reduced when the material is receipted to stock.

- ▶ Consume planning with assembly—This applies to your make-to-order environment, where independent requirements are consumed by the customer order.

- ▶ Consume planning without assembly—This is used for assemble-to-order strategies, where the planning occurs at the component level.

- ▶ Consume planning material without assembly—This type of consumption is used when planning occurs in a material that is used for planning purposes only. The independent requirement for the planning material is consumed when a customer order for an actual finished good related to the planning material is entered. For instance, a dummy material may be created to plan an entire product family. When a customer order is entered for a sellable item in that product family, the independent requirement for the planning material is reduced.

Consumption mode

In a normal make-to-order environment that contains independent requirements, some type of consumption will occur. The method of consumption must be further defined in the consumption mode field of the MRP 3 screen (see Figure 3.4) in the material master. You will need to define whether independent requirements are consumed backwards in time, forwards in time, or a combination of both. For example, if you set the consumption mode to forwards only, planned independent requirements that lie at any date in the past of the customer order entry date will not be consumed.

Planning		
Strategy group		Mixed Planning MTS/MTO
Consumption mode	3	Bwd consumption per.
Fwd consumption per.		Mixed MRP
Planning material		Planning plant
Plng conv. factor		Planning matl BUnit

Figure 3.4: Consumption mode

PLANNING indicator—If a requirements type is maintained for independent requirements, the planning indicator will be predetermined for you based upon the requirements type you select, just like the consumption mode. The choices are:

▶ Net requirements planning—The system takes into account stock and planned goods receipts. This is the most common for make-to-order environments.

▶ Gross requirements planning—The system does not take stock and fixed receipts into account. This is most common in a repetitive make-to-stock environment, where constant production is necessary regardless of the inventory value.

► Single item planning—This type of planning will not consider other materials of the BOM in which the chosen material is structured.

Requirements type of customer requirements

This is the second half of your selected strategy. The selections made in this information set will determine how customer requirements are handled, using some of the same concepts as independent requirements. However, more controls are necessary, since this requirements type must also interpret customer orders and define the results analysis, which determines the method of financial settlement.

REQUIREMENTS TYPE OF CUSTOMER REQUIREMENTS—In this field, your customizer will select the requirements type for your strategy group relevant to customer order entries in MRP. Whether you are in a make-to-stock or make-to-order environment, this requirements type will dictate the planning strategy and financial settlement profile when fulfilling a customer order. There are many standard choices available that contain just about every combination of planning, consumption, and settlement profiles. However, just like the independent requirements type, customized requirements types can be created.

REQUIREMENTS CLASS—As described in the requirements type paragraph above, the requirements class dictates how material costing and financial settlement is to be carried out for the requirements type that has been chosen. More than one requirements type can be assigned to a requirements class.

ALLOCATION indicator—This is very similar to the consumption field that we discussed earlier, with one difference. The setting made in the consumption field will be in regard to planning, whereas the setting made in the allocation indicator looks at consumption from the sales perspective.

NO MRP—In this field, it is decided whether or not the requirement is relevant to MRP planning. You will have three standard choices:

- ▸ Plan the requirement
- ▸ Do not plan the requirement, but display it in MRP
- ▸ Do not plan the requirement, nor display it in MRP

Obviously, the most commonly used choice is to plan the requirement. There are not many cases where you would choose not to do so. At the very least, it is recommended that the requirement be displayed.

ACCOUNT ASSIGNMENT CATEGORY—In this field, you will define what type of account will be assigned to the order for settlement. For example, you can choose to settle costs to a cost center or directly to a sales order.

SETTLEMENT PROFILE—The settlement profile contains the rules for financial settlement. For example, in the settlement profile you can govern which accounts can have a settlement. You can define validity dates of the settlement rule. You can also define split settlement to separate accounts by percentage. The settlement profile is necessary for profitability analysis.

RESULTS ANALYSIS KEY—This field has several different functions depending on the type of order. For instance, if you are settling to a sales order, the results analysis key can be used to valuate stock that has been delivered, but not yet invoiced. If you are not settling to a revenue-based order, such as a production order, the results analysis key will determine how work-in-process is calculated.

AVAILABILITY CHECK indicator—Selecting this indicator will mean that an availability check must occur when the sales order is entered. You can always deselect this indicator in each sales order, but only if it is set as active in the strategy group. If you do not activate this indicator in the strategy group, you do not have the option of turning it on in the sales order.

REQUIREMENT TRANSFER indicator—If this indicator is selected, a transfer of requirements will occur upon sales order entry and an assembly order will be triggered. You can choose to not transfer the requirements in each schedule line of the sales order, but you must have the indicator selected in the strategy group to have that option. Otherwise, no transfer will be performed and you cannot choose to do a transfer of requirements.

REQUIREMENTS REDUCTION indicator—If this indicator is selected, general make-to-stock production requirements will be reduced by the customer order once it is entered.

Assembly order

ASSEMBLY TYPE—This field determines the availability check and procurement process for your assembly orders in an assemble-to-order environment. You will have two choices:

- ▶ Static assembly processing—In this case, there is only one procurement element. The system performs an availability check for components and the procurement element is tied directly to the sales order in question.

- ▶ Dynamic assembly processing—In this case, you are presented with more flexibility. The procurement elements are not tied directly to the sales order. Therefore, you can consider other incoming inventory and place multiple purchase orders with multiple vendors for the same material. However, with this freedom comes a greater risk of human error.

ORDER TYPE—This field allows you to select different order types for your production and processing orders per each strategy group. This allows for specialized financial settlement, amongst other options, that you define in each order type.

ONLINE ASSEMBLY—This option simply allows you to select if you would like to display and/or process missing components when processing your online orders.

CAPACITY CHECK—If the sales order is created online and you are using assembly orders, you can decide to either check for available capacity and schedule according to lead time, or simply schedule to lead time.

COMPONENT AVAILABILITY indicator—If selected, an availability check will occur at the component level during order creation. Depending on your customizing, you may receive a warning or error when components are not available.

Configuration

Configurable materials are common in the assemble-to-order environment. By maintaining a configurable material, you are allowing for different variants of the same material, for instance color choice. A configurable material will have a BOM that contains all components for at least one of the possible variants. The system will check for consistency in planning and settlement once the variant is selected in the final assembly process.

CONFIGURATION—If you are maintaining configurable materials, you must decide whether the configuration is allowed, not allowed, or mandatory in this field.

CONFIGURATION CONSUMPTION—Here is where you define whether your customer requirements will consume independent requirements for either the material variants or conversely the characteristics (i.e. planning material).

3.3 Personal experience

In my personal manufacturing environment experience material lot traceability is of the utmost importance. The products we make must have strict documentation for each material used in the production process. The industry rules dictate that a certification of quality inspection and acceptance, and in some cases the actual inspection results data, must accompany each lot of material. This includes raw materials like fabric and metal and that they be traceable to their origin. Furthermore, as we grew into larger contracting activities with the U.S. government, we found that certain government contracts required that critical components be inspected by a government inspector (DCMA) at various stages of the inspection and assembly process. In those cases, our organization needed to control the batches of inventory that were inspected by the DCMA representative so that we could ensure that the batch of material they inspected was used to build the finished good that would be sold on the contract for which the government representative is responsible.

Up until this point, every batch of a given material we produced was treated exactly the same and could be sold to any customer. Therefore, we had a basic make-to-stock planning strategy entered as our default in

SAP. This strategy worked well up until this point, but did not offer the new requirements control now needed.

This presented us with a difficult problem. Our understanding of SAP's planning strategy was all but non-existent. We did not have a systematic approach to the problem. We began tracking inventory on external spreadsheets because we didn't know another way to do so. Inevitably, mistakes were made in this ad hoc process and high-level corrective actions were issued by our DCMA representative, costing us valuable customer satisfaction performance.

We knew that a systematic approach was available in SAP; we just didn't know how to get there. So, we turned to the consulting world for an up-close and personal education. Very quickly, we were educated on the different aspects of planning strategies and requirements types and our problem was soon solved. We found that by implementing the requirements type sales order with consumption (KSV), along with a few other parameter tweaks to particular product families, MRP would peg our production and procurement lot for lot to the relevant sales order. Thereby ensuring that each lot of material procured or sub-component produced would be dynamically linked to the intended sales order. The benefits of this implementation were great. We could trust that the automatic pegging would resolve the traceability issue and no further manual effort would be required.

This was a perfect example of precise customizing to meet a particular organization's needs. It sounds simple now, but we could not have arrived at this solution without some form of education on SAP planning strategies. The many choices available to you can be very complex due to the nature of the interrelated settings within each strategy and their far-reaching consequences. If you are going to make changes to your planning strategy, I recommend that you have a good understanding of these concepts before attempting any changes. Attempt changes slowly. Take them one at a time, and perform several rounds of testing in your development client to ensure a proper fit for all scenarios before activating the strategy change in your live system.

4 Basic information

In this chapter, I will begin to define the particular screens of the material master and the fields within them. The basic information screens are used to establish a given material's general characteristics.

Now that you have an understanding of material master terminology, standard creation, and points of access, let's turn to the screens within the material master for an in-depth look at each. I will discuss the information sets within each screen and explore each field in depth.

This chapter will focus on the basic data that helps to specify your material. In order to plan, procure, produce, manage, sell, and ship any material, it must be defined by some basic parameters. For instance, what unit of measure will the material be stored in? How will it be transported? Is it too heavy or too large for standard courier services? Is it a dangerous substance? Must the item be classified into a group of similar materials? The BASIC INFORMATION section of the material master will address these concerns. By defining the basics of your material, anyone viewing the material master can get an idea of what type of material it is and how to handle most of its logistics.

4.1 Basic material information

The basic defining attributes of a material master are entered into three screens, normally placed at the beginning of the list of screens. Those screens are BASIC DATA 1, BASIC DATA 2, and CLASSIFICATION. Information in this section will include methods of sub-classifying your material, units of measure, weights, dimensions, and environmental information amongst other relevant information. If your organization wishes to control access to certain aspects of the material master, that authorization can be defined in this section. Most fields contained in these three screens are defined globally, so the entries made within them will apply to all plants across the organization.

4.2   Basic data 1 screen

As the title suggests, the BASIC DATA 1 screen (see Figure 4.1) is where the most basic information about a material is stored. This information is normally defined by someone who initiates material masters for an entire organization and it generally does not change very much over time. There are five information sets within this screen: GENERAL DATA, MATERIAL AUTHORIZATION GROUP, DIMENSIONS/EANs, PACKAGING MATERIAL DATA, and BASIC DATA TEXTS. General data is just that, general information about the material in the entire organization. The material authorization information set can be used to restrict access to certain elements. Information contained within dimensions/EANs is used for storage and transportation. The packaging material data can assist in identifying packaging materials. Finally, the basic data texts information set allows you to store relevant basic material information in languages of your choice.

Figure 4.1: Basic data 1 screen

4.2.1 General data

BASE UNIT OF MEASURE—The base unit of measure is the overall unit of measure used to manage the stock of a particular material within your organization. A material that is purchased in another unit of measure is converted to the base unit of measure upon goods receipt. This allows for consistency in controlling inventory levels. The base unit of measure is most likely defined by someone who controls the overall stock keeping unit and it is managed at the global level. It is most likely managed by an IT technician, MRP controller, master scheduler, or inventory control personnel, which means that the decision of what the base unit of measure might be is out of your control if you are a buyer or planner. It is the responsibility of the individual who decides on the base unit of measure to choose a unit of measure that will define the material in the most precise manner possible, as this unit of measure will be the common denominator to which all alternate units of measure will convert to. This field is also displayed throughout many of the planning and procurement screens of the material master for reference.

MATERIAL GROUP—This field is used to group classes of material together that share similar characteristics. It may not be necessary to maintain this field if you are a business that is not diverse in its product structure, or a business that does not maintain many stock keeping units. The benefit of this field is that it allows you to refine the scope of your reports to specific types of materials that are not already sub-classified by some other means within SAP, for instance, BOM structure. This allows for analysis on those materials by reporting on only the material group that the relevant materials exist in. To use this field effectively, a material group hierarchy must be created to maintain each group. Although you can maintain material groups without a hierarchy, you will not receive the benefits of the material group relationships if you choose not to maintain it. This field is maintained globally, so the hierarchy logic will apply to all plants within the organization.

OLD MATERIAL NUMBER—This is simply a reference field to capture a link to historical or offline information. For example, if you've managed a particular item under a certain part number in your legacy system and have enacted a new numbering scheme upon implementation of SAP, you may wish to insert the old part number for reference. The field is maintained globally, so be sure that the reference applies to all plants within the company.

External Material Group—This field works very much the same as the material group, but the intended application is for grouping materials according to an outside influence.

Case example: External material group

 The Pure Metals Corporation is a distributor of various metal bar, tube, and wire, all of which is managed under one division. However, due to the many different products offered to the public, each of the product families, bar, tube, and wire, are managed by separate functional groups of individuals. The products within the three families have both common and unique ingredients in their respective BOM structures. The head of operations at The Pure Metals Corporation wants to capitalize on the buying power for the various ingredients, such as raw aluminum, required to make the products. In order to do this, she must monitor a different market index pertaining to each raw ingredient. The daily price fluctuations of such materials can be quite volatile according to the stock market and require intense analysis. This concentrated effort requires that forecast reports be generated on products offered by the company every day, according to their respective indices. The individuals tasked with creating these reports have been working around the clock to analyze huge amounts of data that have historically contained irrelevant information. They have given notice that the reports will no longer be completed on time given the current status of the information available to them. The company decides to take action by sub-classifying their materials according to their market indices by creating external material groups for each market index. This way, reports can be generated for products according to the index in which they belong, thereby greatly reducing the reporting effort.

Division—This is yet another way to sub-classify material. Because a material can be assigned to only one division, the field is maintained globally. The purpose of this field is to sub-divide products by sales area. This allows for individuals experienced in sales and distribution of a certain type of product to focus only on that product family or type.

LABORATORY/DESIGN OFFICE—This is a globally maintained field where the design/lab employee or design/lab group can be listed. This can aid others in the organization when they are seeking a contact for design changes and questions. It also helps those in design maintain lists and reports of the items for which they are responsible. The lists of entries for this field must be maintained in SAP customizing before they are available for selection in the material master. Note: In the example provided (see Figure 4.1), this field is titled ADR due to a custom need within my organization.

PRODUCT ALLOCATION—This is a globally maintained field. Maintaining this field allows for a more sophisticated availability check during sales and planning procedures. In SAP customizing, you can create product allocation determining procedures that contain one or more objects with validity dates. If you assign one of those allocation procedures to a material, the system will apply the appropriate object, and therefore availability check, by using the object whose validity date corresponds with the order due date. The ability to assign several objects to one allocation procedure allows for a refined availability check. However, there are two main types of allocation determining procedures, which are chosen in SAP customizing. These choices will be built in to the choices available to you in the material master:

- ▶ Discrete—In this case, allocation checks will only evaluate available quantities within the proposed order period, and disregard remaining available quantities from previous periods.

- ▶ Cumulated—This type of allocation procedure will include remaining available quantities from previous periods during the availability check.

PRODUCT HIERARCHY—This is a globally maintained field used for competitive analysis. The purpose of this field is to create a product structure consisting of materials with similar characteristics. This allows for a comparison of price between your company's items and those of competitors. For this to be effective, you must maintain competitive materials (materials created to simulate your competitor's items, using material type WETT). You can have up to three levels of product in the hierarchy. For instance, you might have level 1 (code 0007) as electronics, level 2 (code 00A) as televisions, and level 3 (code 004) as plasma televisions. Therefore, your product hierarchy code for a plasma TV would be

0000700A004. Unless you are in a highly competitive market, you will most likely not maintain this field.

CROSS-PLANT MATERIAL STATUS—This globally maintained field is used to apply restrictions to a material across all plants within the organization. You can prohibit materials for use for procurement, planning, inventory movements, and costing by applying choices in this field. You can further extend the use of this field by applying your own restrictions in SAP customizing. This field can be very useful in a large organization, where restrictions on materials must be communicated effectively and instantly. In the following chapters, I will explain how you can restrict material on a plant by plant basis.

VALID FROM—The date you input in this field will control the timing of implementation of your chosen cross-plant material status. If you input the date February 1st in this field, the intended restriction will not apply to transactions processed for the given material on January 31st.

Case example: Cross-plant material status

 The Alpha Dog Motorcycle Company produces motorcycles for customers across the globe. They are centrally controlled and have 16 manufacturing and assembly plants in North America and Europe. Quality is high at Alpha Dog, but every motorcycle company experiences a need for product recall from time to time. The recall process can be expensive and Alpha Dog wants to limit the amount of financial loss that occurs. Senior leadership has identified one possible way to curtail recall costs. They must find a way to immediately stop production of the component being recalled to prevent their facilities from producing items that are potentially scrap. The company decides to use the cross-plant material status as their means of control. They use the abilities within SAP customizing to develop their own status, which is titled "product recall." This feature allows the head of the quality department to enact an immediate stoppage of work on a given recalled item in all plants across the globe by installing procurement, planning, and inventory blocks within their product recall material status. Once the status is set, the item will no longer be able to be used in production or inventory transactions until the block is lifted.

GENERAL ITEM CATEGORY GROUP—This globally maintained field is used to classify a material for consideration in sales documents. For instance, you can categorize an item as make-to-order, which will cause a sales document to require that a delivery transaction be processed to relieve inventory. Conversely, you can select the item category service, which does not require a delivery transaction when processing a sale because no physical good is being shipped. In the latter case, you can create an invoice directly from the sales document.

4.2.2 Material authorization group

AUTHORIZATION GROUP—This global field is fairly straightforward. If you are maintaining authorization groups, you can assign individuals to a given group. Once that group is selected in this field for a material, only those individuals within the group may make changes to the material master and/or make changes to batch records, depending on the settings you choose for the group.

Restrict material master maintenance in large or data-sensitive organizations

 If you are in an environment where many individuals have access to SAP, I recommend that you restrict material master maintenance. By nature, people are curious about systematic settings. If they are not educated on the matter, individuals may try their hand at making changes to a material master just for the sake of learning, or perhaps they feel that they have an understanding, when in fact, they do not. Unless the authorization is restricted, you may find critical and sensitive data changed by a curious employee, causing unimaginable disaster in your MRP system. While general authorizations are controlled within each employee's login profile, maintaining authorization groups can help to refine certain authorizations in regard to material master maintenance by defining exactly who is authorized for the function.

4.2.3 Dimensions/EANs

GROSS WEIGHT—In this globally maintained field, you can express the weight of one unit of a material as it will be stored or shipped. That is, the gross weight includes the material as well as the packaging it is contained in.

If you are using advanced warehouse management practices, SAP can use the gross weight to check storage bin capacity for material stocking activities. Gross weight can also be used in processing delivery transactions to determine packaging criteria.

NET WEIGHT—In this field, you can store the weight of one unit of the material only. This field is globally maintained.

WEIGHT UNIT—In order to use the gross weight or the net weight fields, you must maintain a weight unit. For instance, kilogram may be used as a weight unit, so if the base unit of measure is meter, then the value you enter in the either weight field will be expressed as kilograms per meter.

You must maintain a weight unit for sales transactions. Be sure you are selecting the appropriate unit as this field is also stored in the SALES screen, which is copied into the sales order upon creation and cannot be changed there.

Use gross weight to ensure safety in your warehouse

 If you are using storage racks to store your heavier items in inventory, those racks will be the defining limit of your storage capacity in space, but more importantly in weight. Storage racks are only certified to a certain maximum weight capacity. By maintaining gross weight values, you can ensure that you never exceed your storage racks' maximum capacity. Therefore, you will be protecting yourself against potentially dangerous and costly accidents.

VOLUME—Just as with gross weight, volume can be useful for evaluating storage capacity. The only difference is that the storage capacity is evaluated by dimension rather than weight. This field is also globally maintained.

VOLUME UNIT—Maintaining a value for volume requires that you define its unit of measure, just as gross and net weight do. However, it is not required that you maintain a volume unit for sales transactions.

Use volume to ensure efficiency in your warehouse

 If you have a limited amount of storage space and you are in a growing sales environment, you may be considering purchasing additional storage capacity. If you were to maintain volume values, you may find that you are using your current storage capacity less efficiently than you could. You can use the values in the volume field to define how much space you require. Furthermore, if an expansion is necessary, the values maintained in the volume field can help you to predict the required amount of additional storage space.

SIZE/DIMENSIONS—While this field is globally maintained, it is not used by the system for any type of calculation. The information you enter here is for informational purposes only. SAP recommends that if you enter dimensions in this field that you include the units of measure being used.

EAN/UPC—EAN refers to the internationally used international article number. In the United States, this field refers to the universal product code (UPC). This field is used in SAP to uniquely identify a material's unit of measure or standard packaging. It can either be defined internally by your company, or externally by another industry source.

If you are assigning a numbering system internally, you will enter the EAN category and the international article number will be entered automatically. If the international article number is defined externally, you will select an EAN/UPC and the category will be determined for you. Either option must be maintained in SAP customizing for use.

EAN CATEGORY—When maintaining international article numbers you need not use the entire number. Each portion of the international article number is for certain criteria, such as quality, quantity, and unit packaging. This field determines how an international article number will be assigned internally and which characteristics of the international article number to check for. For example, you may only be interested in checking the unit packaging of the material.

4.2.4   Packaging material data

MATERIAL GROUP: PACKAGING MATERIALS—This globally maintained field is used to enter a type of material group that classifies material by similar packaging materials. For example, you could create a group called "spool" for those items like cable, wire, or rope that need to be wound on a spool for shipment. This would aid you in the ordering process for packaging spools by reporting on the demand of all materials relevant to that material group.

4.2.5   Basic data texts

BASIC DATA TEXT icon—By clicking on this icon, you are taken to the BASIC DATA TEXT field, which is globally maintained. This is a free text box for general information and can be entered in any language that you maintain. The BASIC DATA TEXT is a separate screen that is stored in the additional data screen set. The additional data screens are for supplemental information that you want to maintain for your material master. It can also be accessed by clicking on the ADDITIONAL DATA icon (see Figure 4.2), located on the top of every main material master screen.

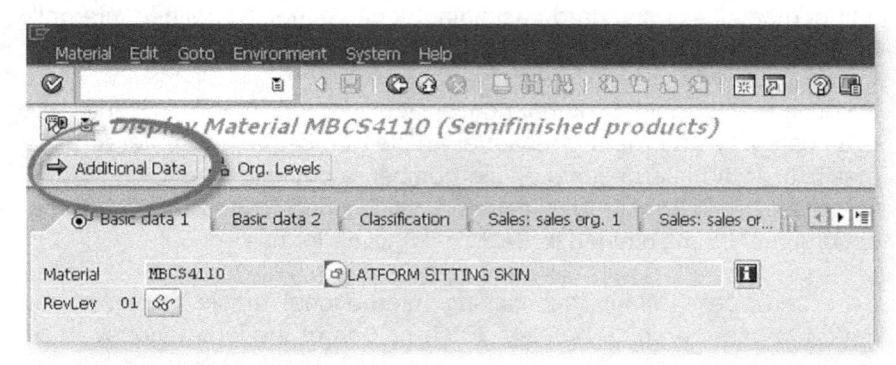

Figure 4.2: Additional Data icon

4.3 Basic data 2 screen

The BASIC DATA 2 screen (see Figure 4.3) is a continuance of the BASIC DATA 1 screen. It contains five information sets: OTHER DATA, ENVIRONMENT, DESIGN DOCUMENTS ASSIGNED, DESIGN DRAWING, and CLIENT-SPECIFIC CONFIGURATION. The information set OTHER DATA contains various, basic information about the material that does not fit into any other category. The fields within the environment information set have to do with shipping and handling hazardous goods. Both the DESIGN DOCUMENTS ASSIGNED and DESIGN DRAWING information sets are for information about the drawing for the material. And finally, CLIENT-SPECIFIC CONFIGURATION is used to maintain materials with variable configurations.

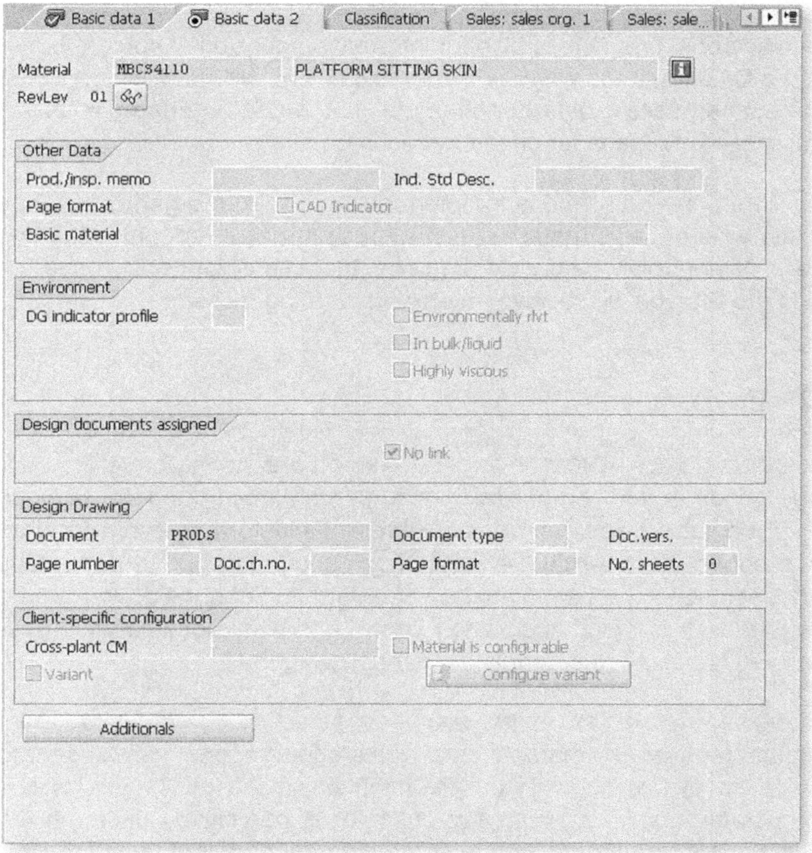

Figure 4.3: Basic data 2 screen

4.3.1 Other data

PRODUCTION/INSPECTION MEMO—This globally maintained field is for information only. You can enter text here to provide a general note or instruction about the material.

INDUSTRY STANDARD DESCRIPTION—This is another information-only screen where you can choose to store the industry standard applicable to the material. For example, ISO9100 may be a choice.

PAGE FORMAT—This informational screen is used to specify the paper size to be used for a memo. Certain industry standards call for documentation to be printed on a certain size paper.

CAD indicator—This field is also for information only, but if you are maintaining a CAD interface with SAP, this indicator will be checked if a linked document has been created or changed via the CAD interface. It can be useful in search criteria for changed documents.

BASIC MATERIAL—This field is for information only. Your organization may maintain a list of basic materials in SAP customizing. If so, any entry you make in this field will be checked against that list. If your entry does not exist in the list, you will receive an error or warning message.

4.3.2 Environment

DANGEROUS GOODS INDICATOR PROFILE—If you are storing or selling dangerous goods in your organization, you can maintain dangerous goods profiles. Those profiles can contain several indicators: relevant for dangerous goods, execute dangerous goods check, and output dangerous goods document. By maintaining a value in this global field, you will be telling the system which checks to perform and what documents to generate when shipping and handling a dangerous good.

ENVIRONMENTALLY RELEVANT indicator—By selecting this indicator, environmental reports, like material safety data sheet reports, can be sent to the receiver of this good if you are maintaining the necessary data in SAP customizing. Maintaining this indicator is particularly useful in the industrial chemical market, where environmental data is a legal shipping and receiving requirement.

> ## Use the environmentally relevant indicator to drive modern supply chain success
>
>  A growing trend amongst supply chain professionals is to focus on what experts refer to as *The Triple Bottom Line*. The Triple Bottom Line (TBL) refers to focusing on three major factors that drive organizational sustainability. The three elements are economic, social, and environmental. The environmental aspect of TBL often involves educating product users on how to return, reuse, repair, or recycle the items you've sold them. There can be significant financial benefit to being environmentally friendly if your solution involves returning and repairing for profit or selling maintenance materials to the user. If you are interested in pursuing something like this, using the ENVIRONMENTALLY RELEVANT indicator to automatically distribute the return or repair instructions is a nice touch.

IN BULK/LIQUID indicator—This indicator will also drive output documentation if you are maintaining the necessary data in SAP customizing. By selecting this indicator, you are informing the output report that this item is being shipped in bulk. This indicator can prompt specific hazard codes within the output report.

HIGHLY VISCOUS indicator—Just like the bulk/liquid indicator, by selecting this indicator you are driving additional information about the danger of the material into the output report created during delivery.

4.3.3   Design documents assigned

DOCUMENT LINK indicator—This indicator will be checked if you are maintaining document links of any kind to the material master.

4.3.4   Design drawing

This information set can be used when you are not maintaining a document management system that is linked to the material master. Each of the fields within this information set is for informational purposes only, although some of the data entered will be displayed in certain report lists.

4.3.5 Client-specific configuration

This information set is useful in the assemble-to-order environment, where the same product is available with a few different attributes to choose from. SAP refers to this as a configurable material. A configurable material is one whose attributes can vary within the same material master. For example, a shirt may be available in four different colors, but maintains only one material number. There are two types of configurable materials: cross-plant materials and plant-specific materials. This information set controls cross-plant configurable materials, which is valid for use in all plants within the organization.

CROSS-PLANT CONFIGURABLE MATERIAL—This globally maintained field is where the alphanumeric configurable material number is entered.

CONFIGURABLE MATERIAL indicator—By selecting this indicator, you are saying that it is possible for this material to have variants. If you do not have the ability to change this indicator, it is because the indicator has been predetermined for you in SAP customizing by the material type you are using.

MATERIAL IS A VARIANT indicator—By selecting this indicator, you are saying that this material is one variant of another configurable material. For this to be possible, this material must be listed as a variant in the characteristics of the configurable material. The purpose for doing this is so that you can stock a commonly used variant as its own unique material number in advance of a demand requirement.

CONFIGURE VARIANT icon—By clicking this icon you will be taken to a screen where you can define the variants of the configurable material.

4.4 Classification screen

The CLASSIFICATION screen (see Figure 4.4) is where you can view all class types assigned to your material. In each class type, you can define the specific attributes of your material, called characteristics. The amount of information stored here is limited to the characteristics assigned to each of your material classes. Material classes are defined in SAP customizing and their characteristics are specific to your environment. The purpose of classifying material is to shorten your search for any given item, by restricting the search to the item's material class. You will also have the benefit of defining the material in great detail.

In my facility, we only maintain one general class (see Figure 4.4), which contains several characteristics, for example, National Stock Number. However, you have the ability to maintain several different classes, each of which can have their own characteristics. Maintaining these characteristics will help you if you are using configurable materials.

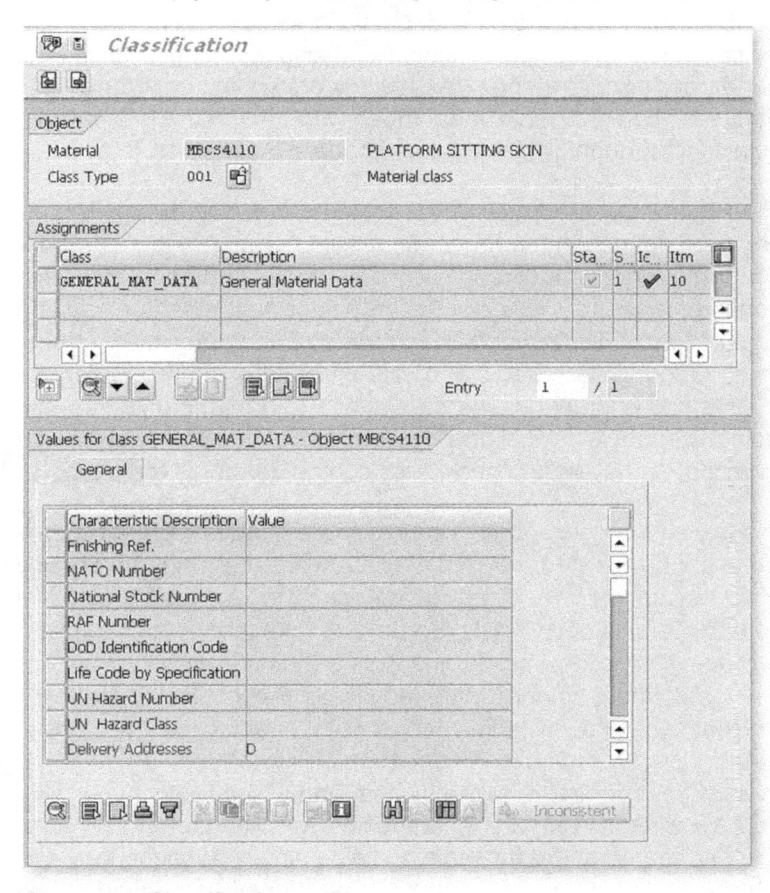

Figure 4.4: Classification screen

4.5 Personal experience

Fortunately, my experience with the material master in relation to the basic information screens has been one of measured control. I work for a production plant in the United States that supports a larger organization in the United Kingdom, where the corporate headquarters reside. The design offices for all of the organization's plants are located at the corporate headquarters. Consequently, the SAP master data is created and entered at that location. Our practice is to create material masters in our plant by copying them from corporate headquarters.

At first I thought, why bother copying this information? There was very little relevant information being copied. Couldn't we just create the material master from scratch (our perspective) and skip all of the adjustments required when performing a copy? As my understanding of the material master matured, I came to realize that those who control the master data had put significant thought into the values that are maintained.

An important factor to our mutual success is the fact that the base units of measure were defined in the broadest possible terms, which allows for all sorts of wiggle room when it comes to differences in procurement and planning units of measure. This can be very important when conducting international business. What works in Europe does not necessarily translate very well to the United States and vice versa. The simplest example of this is converting an imperial unit of measure to a metric unit of measure. A second benefit was that there were predefined material groups and revision control that were a necessary central control of the plants.

While this was all well and good, what eventually gave me high confidence in those who created the master data were the many fields they chose *not* to maintain. Every organization wants to use their expensive ERP system to the best of its ability. Some may take that as an obligation to maintain every possible field so that the greatest possible control is implemented and the company can recognize the greatest return on software investment. However, in many cases, nothing can be further from the truth. It is an organization's responsibility to identify which parameters assist your control over the system and which restrict your ability to conduct business. Too often, companies will overuse an ERP system, only to find that they are maintaining fields simply because they can and feel that they should, when in fact no real benefit is derived. It behooves you to find that balance in what should and should not be maintained, and align your ERP needs to your value stream and legal requirements rather than your urge to fill in blank spaces Besides, it is much easier to refine the material master as new requirements make themselves known, rather than trying to eliminate useless data already in existence.

5 Sales

In this chapter, I will discuss the material master parameters that are used to control how a product is sold and distributed to the customer.

Individuals who work in sales have been known to be rather territorial when it comes to their product family and sales region. This is for good reason. Sales is a highly competitive form of employment, both internal and external to the company. Many people working in sales earn a majority of their salary through commission. For this reason alone, sales representatives want to ensure that credit is received when credit is due. They also want the ability to classify and report on the items they are responsible for in a clear and concise manner. As their main job function, ensuring customer satisfaction is the top priority, so those managing and supporting sales need the ability to finely control product distribution. Fortunately, the SAP Material Master has integration that allows a sales representative to track his or her progress, as well as control parameters to facilitate production scheduling and product distribution.

However, managing the sales parameters in the material master is far more complex than tracking commission and classifying products. As a representative of a sales department, or an employee who is responsible for entering a customer order into SAP, you will find that the settings within the material master affect production scheduling, pricing, taxation, and account settlement amongst other important sales actions. You will also have the ability to restrict certain sales and logistics activities when necessary. The introduction of a customer order into SAP has potentially far reaching impact into MRP and related SAP logistics features. After all, it is the customer order that initiates the majority of your systematic demand. For this reason, this chapter has been written from the perspective of those entering customer orders, as well as the individuals managing MRP, to which the settings of the sales area of the material master will apply.

In this chapter, I will discuss the settings within the sales area of the material master and how they can be used to fine tune scheduling and automate other activities, like applying a cash discount for early payment.

5.1 Sales structure in the material master

The screens of the material master pertaining to sales are managed a bit differently than other functional areas. While there are both global and plant-specific fields, you will be maintaining each material according to a particular sales area. A sales area is made up of a combination of sales organization, plant, and distribution channel. This type of classification allows for product responsibility to be assigned to individuals or groups based on legal liability and distribution methods. Therefore, when you are accessing one of the five sales area material master screens, you will be presented with the following screen (see Figure 5.1) to specify the sales area you are interested in. Here, you will need to enter the relevant plant, sales organization, and distribution channel.

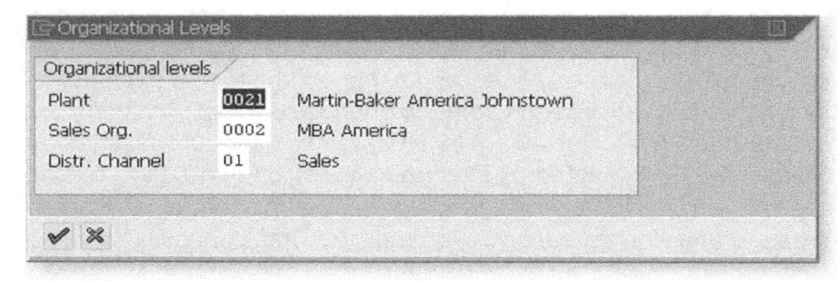

Figure 5.1: Sales area

There are five screens related to sales and distribution activities in the material master. They are: SALES ORGANIZATION 1, SALES ORGANIZATION 2, SALES GENERAL / PLANT, FOREIGN TRADE EXPORT, and SALES TEXT. It should be noted that the steps required to enter a customer order and maintain the relevant material master settings are truly part of the sales and operations planning process. A sales and operations planning process is not an SAP function, but an external planning format based on cross-functional communication. Because sales and operations planning is an intense team effort that requires continuous attention, I recommend that your sales and operations planning procedures are documented in detail to include the intended SAP Material Master settings.

5.2 Sales organization 1 screen

The SALES ORGANIZATION 1 screen (see Figure 5.2) has three information sets: GENERAL DATA, TAX DATA, and QUANTITY STIPULATIONS. The fields within these information sets can help you control material availability for distribution channels, automate tax calculations, and specify parameters for sales quantities.

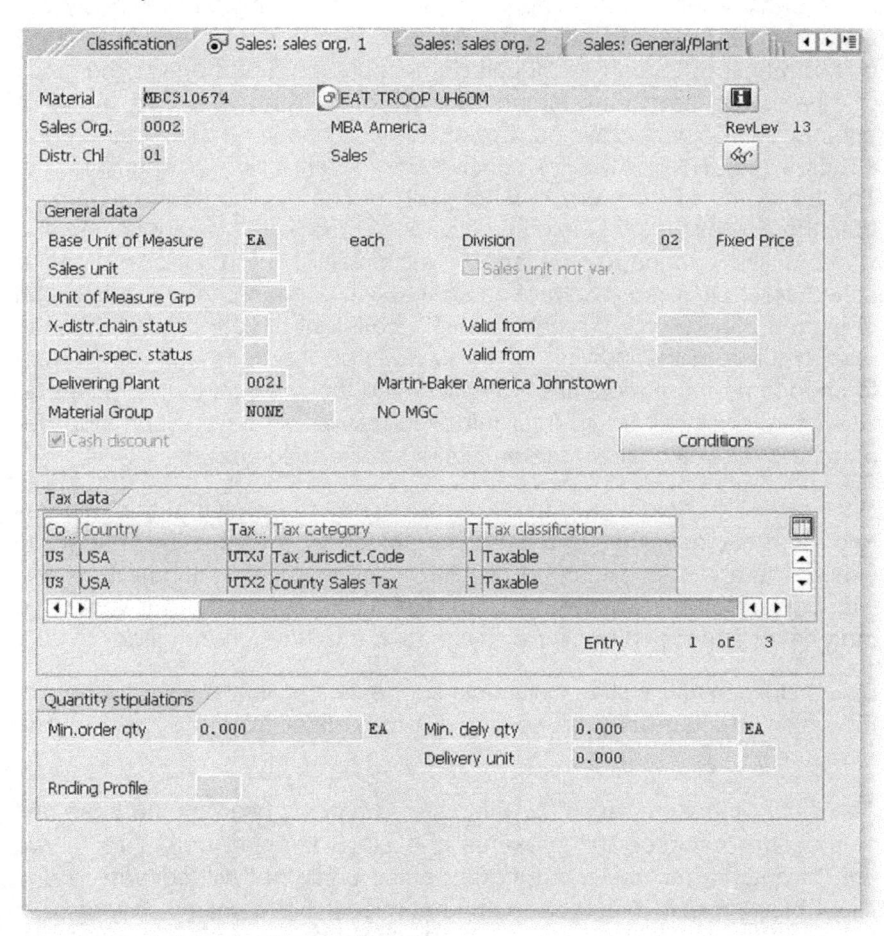

Figure 5.2: Sales organization 1 screen

5.2.1 General data

The fields contained within this information set will help you to assign your material to a particular sales unit and otherwise classify your material. In this information set, you can also define the terms of any cash discount you are willing to provide to your customers.

BASE UNIT OF MEASURE—This is the same field that was previously defined in Chapter 4, but has been included here for reference. The base unit of measure is the overall unit of measure used to manage the stock of a particular material within your organization. A material that is sold in another unit of measure is converted from the base unit of measure upon goods issue. This allows for consistency in controlling inventory levels. The base unit of measure is most likely defined by someone who controls the overall stock keeping unit, and is managed at the global level. It is most likely managed by an IT technician, MRP controller, master scheduler, or inventory control personnel, which means that the decision of what the base unit of measure might be is out of your control. It is the responsibility of the individual who decides on the base unit of measure to choose a unit of measure that will define the material in the most precise manner possible, as this unit of measure will be the common denominator to which all alternate units of measure convert to.

DIVISION—This field allows for materials in any given distribution channel to be further classified into a particular category. The intention is to group similar materials in the same division in order to align those materials with personnel who possess the appropriate expertise. For this reason, a material or service can only be assigned to one division at a time.

SALES UNIT—As the title of this field suggests, this is the unit of measure for which the item may be sold and it may differ from the base unit of measure.

The unit of measure, each (EA), is very commonly used for the base unit of measure because it represents one stock keeping unit. This allows you to enter a multitude of different sales units that will convert to one stock keeping unit. The relationship between the two units is managed in the general conversion table in SAP. For instance, you may produce construction aggregate and stock it by the pound (LB). However, it is your company's intention to sell the aggregate by the ton (TON). In this case, the base unit of measure is (LB), and you would enter (TON) into the sales unit field. Now, each time a delivery is created in SAP, it will be proposed per ton of aggregate. You will still have the opportunity to change the unit of measure in the delivery, if you so desire, as long as you have not selected the SALES UNIT NOT VARIABLE indicator in the material master.

SALES UNIT NOT VARIABLE indicator—By selecting this indicator, you are stating that the sales unit may not vary from what is stored in the material master in related delivery transactions. This field is useful when segregating distribution channels.

Case example: Sales unit

 The Green Leaves Tea Company bottles specialty iced teas for two distribution channels. One type of distribution is through Green Leaves Tea Company sales representatives, who receive the iced tea by the case and sell individual bottles of iced tea on the street from a refrigerated cart. The other method involves selling pallets of cases of bottles to a wholesaler for further distribution. The result is a cheaper price per bottle to the wholesaler who buys the tea by the pallet, where the price break occurs. Although The Green Leaves Tea Company has stated to their employees that cases should be sold to the company's sales reps and pallets should be sold to the wholesaler, they have found that their instructions are not being followed Senior leadership has discovered that sales reps order pallets of bottles to receive the discounted rate, and conversely, wholesalers order a single case to obtain a smaller quantity of a flavor that does not sell quickly. Luckily, this problem can easily be resolved through material master maintenance. The Green Leaves Tea Company decides to assign the sales unit case (CS) to the sales area containing the direct sales distribution channel and the sales unit pallet (PAL) to the sales area containing the wholesale distribution channel. In each of the sales areas, the company selects the SALES UNIT NOT VARIABLE indicator. This activity, combined with authorization restrictions on material master maintenance, effectively eliminates the unwanted distribution.

UNIT OF MEASURE GROUP—This field allows you to assign a group of allowable units of measure for a particular material. This can aide in restricting how a material may be sold, but more importantly, this field must be maintained if "check customer" is selected when maintaining a rounding profile. In this case, the rounding profile will seek the allowable units of measure to form its calculation.

DISTRIBUTION CHAIN MATERIAL STATUS—A distribution chain consists of a sales organization and distribution channel. There are two types of material status that can be applied to your distribution chain, and each requires that a validity date be applied (see Figure 5.2). The material status applied to the cross-distribution chain field will restrict the material for all distribution chains within the organization according to the rules of the status that you apply. The material status applied to the distribution chain-specific field will only apply to the sales distribution chain for the sales area you are maintaining. The statuses that you can apply to each field will have the ability to restrict activities related to sales documents. For instance, you may block a material for sale that is currently experiencing a non-conformance by applying the material status "technical defect."

Use distribution chain material status to control the release of new products

 If you are in a company where new products are developed and later released for sale, you will need a mechanism to control that release. When a company designs a new product, it is necessary to begin building the SAP planning structure before the item can enter production and become ready for sale. By applying a restrictive material status such as "under development" to the distribution chain, you will have the ability to create new component materials, BOM and routing structures, procure component materials, and even stock the final product while enjoying the assurance that the final product will not be released for sale until the status has been removed. This can be a very useful tool in your sales and operations planning procedure.

Advanced tip: Use distribution chain material status to avoid overbooking

 While a healthy amount of backlog may keep an organization motivated, too much backlog is likely to cause delays in delivery. The costs of these delays add up when you consider the potential for lost customers or the cost of overtime to get back on schedule. Backlog can grow quickly, particularly when sales teams are compensated by commission. Why should the salesperson care how production meets demand? Their pay is based on as many sales as possible. In order to prevent overbooking by a salesperson, you may consider using the distribution chain material status to block the entry of new sales until adequate capacity is available again. Furthermore, you can report on materials blocked by the distribution chain material status as a talking point in your sales and operations planning meetings, where focus can be placed on items that have the potential for more sales by increasing capacity or some other mitigation that is appropriate for the sales and operations planning (S&OP) meeting.

DELIVERING PLANT—As I stated previously in this chapter, a sales area is created with a combination of three required components: a sales organization, a plant, and a distribution channel. However, it is possible to deliver inventory from a plant other than that which the sales area was created for. The plant that you apply to this field will be the plant that is defaulted into sales documents. You will still have the ability to amend the default delivery plant in the sales document if you so desire.

> ## Default entries can be proposed by several different areas of SAP
>
>  You may find that you have chosen not to maintain a certain field in the material master, yet you are seeing default values being proposed into the related field within your respective documents. The reason for this is that some document field default values can be suggested from several different sources, some of which are outside of the material master. The delivery plant field is a good example. The delivery plant can be suggested in sales documents from either the material master, or the customer master. It all depends on where you choose to maintain the value. In most cases, there is a hierarchy in place to decide which field will take precedence in the event you are maintaining the field in more than one area of the system.

MATERIAL GROUP—This is the same field that was discussed in Chapter 4, under the BASIC DATA 1 screen. It is also listed here for reference.

CASH DISCOUNT indicator—By selecting this indicator, you are saying that the sale of this material can qualify for a cash discount. This type of discount is normally given for early payment. The precise terms of the applicable cash discount must be defined in the financial accounting module within SAP customizing.

CONDITIONS icon—If you are maintaining a cash discount, the terms of your discount for a given material can be seen by clicking this icon.

5.2.2   Tax data

In this information set, you can specify whether or not taxes should apply to the item upon sale. You can maintain a different tax rule for each applicable tax. For instance at my organization, we maintain three separate tax rules: federal, state, and local taxes. By marking the rule that has been created as taxable in the material master, you are saying that the tax rates entered in the financial accounting module of SAP are applied to the sale of the given material.

5.2.3 Quantity stipulations

MINIMUM ORDER QUANTITY—The value you enter in this field will be the minimum quantity that the customer is allowed to order. Any entry you make in a sales document for the given item at a lesser quantity will be presented with an error message.

MINIMUM DELIVERY QUANTITY—The value you enter here will be the minimum quantity allowed in any delivery created for the given material. This is useful when you are often making partial deliveries against a large quantity order. By implementing a minimum delivery quantity, you are going to reduce the frequency of shipments and hopefully, overall shipping costs for the order. It should be noted that the maximum number of partial deliveries can be defined for an order by maintaining that value in the customer master. You may want to consider how many partial deliveries are allowed before setting your minimum delivery quantity.

DELIVERY UNIT—This field can be used to specify a multiple for the quantities that you want to deliver in. The field also requires that you maintain a unit of measure. For instance, you can define the unit of measure as feet (FT) and the delivery unit quantity as (20). In this case the system will allow deliveries of (20) feet, (40) feet, (60) feet, etc. However, by maintaining the values in this example, you will be prevented from delivering in any other multiple, for instance (75) feet.

ROUNDING PROFILE—This field is a more sophisticated version of maintaining the delivery unit field. The rounding profile is used to propose deliverable quantities in the sales order. If you are using a static rounding profile, that rounding profile can also be used to guide requirements planning. This is another case where information can be derived from two different parts of the material master. If you are interested in maintaining rounding parameters for requirements planning, you can either maintain a static rounding profile in this field or maintain a rounding value in the lot size data information set of the MRP 1 screen (see Section 7.2.3). Be aware that the rounding profile field in the SALES ORGANIZATION 1 screen takes precedence over the rounding value in the MRP 1 screen.

If you choose to maintain a rounding profile, you will have three choices for rounding profile types. The parameters of each profile are defined in SAP customizing. The three rounding profile types are:

▶ Static—This type of profile requires a threshold value. If the requirement value exceeds the threshold value, the proposed quantity is rounded up to the next multiple as defined in the profile. If the requirement value is below the threshold, you are simply given the actual requirement value.

▶ Dynamic—This rounding profile uses layers of delivery units. For instance, if you have thirty bottles in a case, and someone orders forty-five bottles, the system will propose the delivery unit of two cases. Be aware that you cannot control requirements planning with this type of profile, only delivery quantities.

▶ With quantity added/subtracted—In this case, the requirements quantity is either increased or decreased based on a defined percentage. Be aware that you cannot control requirements planning with this type of profile, only delivery quantities.

Note: This field is cross-functional

If you are maintaining a static rounding profile from a sales perspective, you will want to ensure that the profile makes sense to those individuals maintaining requirements planning. This is yet another reason to include your system settings in the sales and operations planning process.

5.3   Sales organization 2 screen

The SALES ORGANIZATION 2 screen (see Figure 5.3) contains two information sets: GROUPING TERMS and PRODUCT ATTRIBUTES. The fields within the grouping terms information set allow you to apply materials to group codes that affect pricing and financial settlement. The product attribute information set is used to restrict materials from being delivered to customers who do not desire products with certain features.

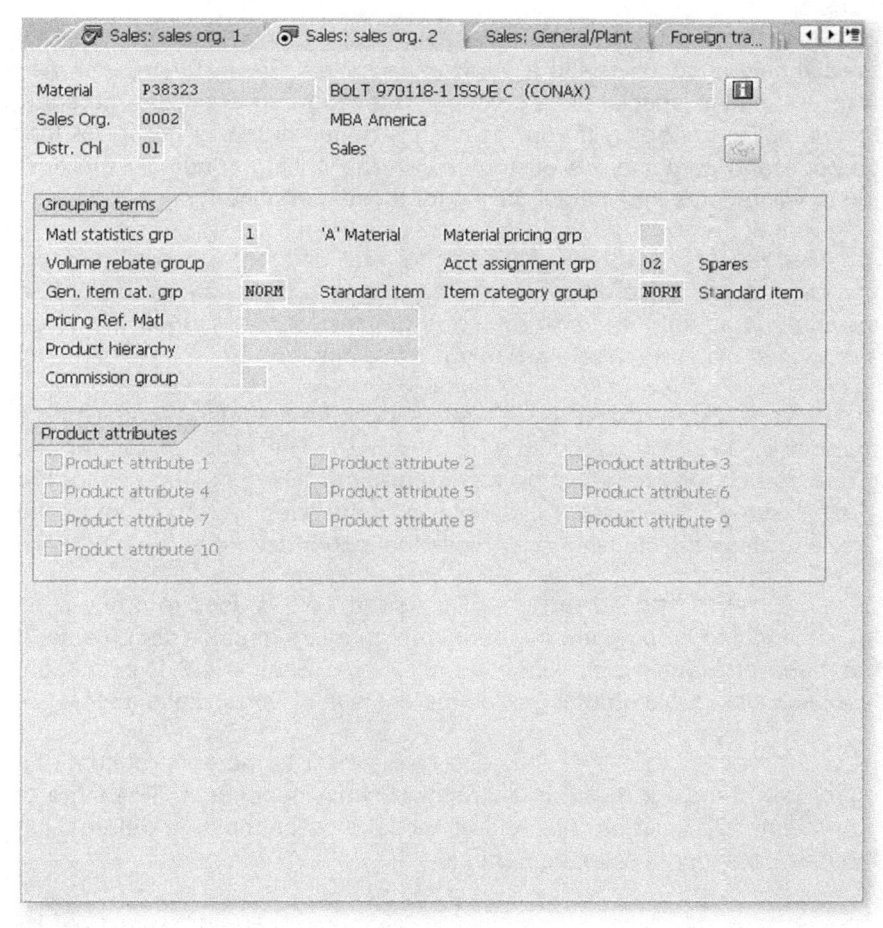

Figure 5.3: Sales organization 2 screen

5.3.1 Grouping terms

MATERIAL STATISTICS GROUP—By maintaining material statistics groups, you can define in SAP customizing which data categories are updated in the logistics information system for statistical analysis when the material is sold. The possible categories to include in a material statistics group are the item category, sales document type, customer, and material.

MATERIAL PRICING GROUP—You maintain material pricing groups to apply special pricing conditions to a particular element. For instance, you may want to apply a special pricing condition for a group of similar materials to a specific customer. If you maintain a material pricing group for that purpose and combine the customer with the pricing condition, the customer will receive the special pricing for those components.

VOLUME REBATE GROUP—If you offer several different types of rebates, you can assign those different rebates to a volume rebate group. When the material is sold, a credit memo is generated based upon the value stored in the volume rebate group you have applied.

ACCOUNT ASSIGNMENT GROUP—This is simply the field used to assign the material to a revenue account when it is sold. The account assignment group you choose here will be carried into the billing documents for the given material. The choices available will be defined for you by someone in financial controlling who determines the ledger accounts.

GENERAL ITEM CATEGORY GROUP—This global field is used to group similar materials to help determine their item category in sales documents. It has been previously defined in Chapter 4 (see Section 4.2.1) because it is a basic data function that groups materials at an organizational level.

ITEM CATEGORY GROUP—This field is very similar to the general item category group except that it is distribution chain dependent. Therefore, if you maintain a value in this field, it will take precedence in determining the item category in sales documents.

An item category is used to define the attributes of an item within a document. For instance, if you are selling a service, you will want the item category for the corresponding sales document line item to be relevant to the characteristics of a service. This means that the item category will allow you to ignore the delivery processing part of a sales document, because there is no physical item to deliver when selling a service. Furthermore, a service type of item category will not look for inventory to deliver. Conversely, an item category that is used for the normal selling of materials will require a delivery transaction from inventory of that material.

PRICING REFERENCE MATERIAL—By entering another material number in this field, you are telling the system to apply the same pricing rules to the given material you are maintaining. This is useful when you want to apply the same pricing to two materials, but you do not want to maintain a material pricing group for one or both materials.

PRODUCT HIERARCHY—This field was previously defined in Chapter 4 (see Section 4.2.1). However, the field in the BASIC DATA 1 screen is applied globally. The setting that you apply here is for your own sales organization and will override any entry made in the BASIC DATA 1 screen.

COMMISSION GROUP—For you sales representatives, this is the field you may be most concerned with. This field assigns materials to a commission group to which sales representatives are assigned. The specifics of the commission are assigned by percentage in the representative's profile. The key is that each representative in the group must get the same percentage for each material to which the commission group is assigned. However that percentage can vary between each sales representative. See Figure 5.4 for a visual explanation. By assigning commission groups to materials, sales representatives have a link to the materials for which they are responsible. With this link, various reporting features are now available to those concerned with their sales data.

Material	Rep A	Rep B	Rep C
X003	3%	7%	4%
A211	3%	7%	4%
V312	3%	7%	4%

Figure 5.4: Commission group table

5.3.2 Product attributes

A product attribute is a characteristic that is included in a particular material. For example, an attribute of a prepackaged charcoal grill may be that it comes with a complimentary bag of charcoal. You may have a certain distribution customer who does not want the bag of charcoal with the grill. Therefore, you define the charcoal as an attribute of the grill in the material master. You will also define the same attribute in the customer's material master as an attribute that they do not want. Now, when the material is entered into a sales document the system checks to see if the material's defined attribute is allowed by the customer. If it is not, you will be presented with an error message to prevent the shipment of this item.

5.4 Sales: General/Plant screen

The SALES: GENERAL/PLANT screen (see Figure 5.5) contains four information sets: general data, shipping data, packaging material data, and general plant parameters. The fields contained in all four information sets are used to drive the final logistics and shipping functions of a sale.

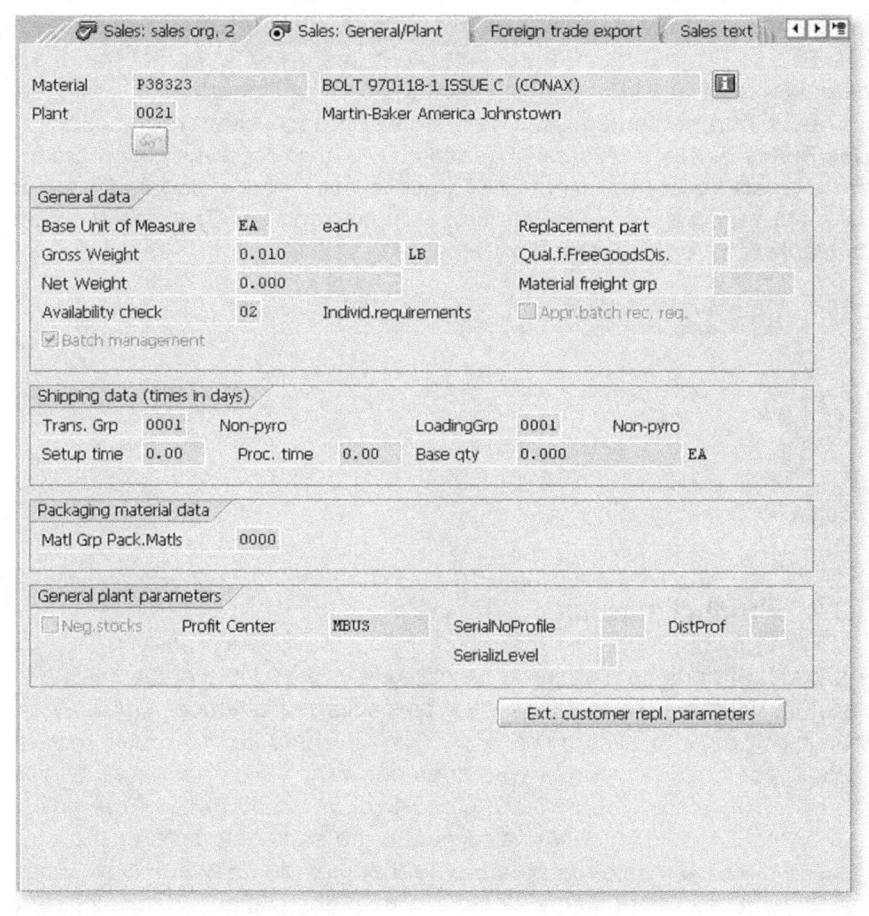

Figure 5.5: Sales: General/Plant screen

5.4.1 General data

BASE UNIT OF MEASURE—This is the same field that has been described in the general data information set of the SALES ORGANIZATION 1 screen (see Section 5.2.1). It has been included here for its application to both gross and net weight.

GROSS WEIGHT—This is the same field that was described in the BASIC DATA 1 screen (see Section 4.2.3). It has been included here for its application to shipping.

NET WEIGHT—This is also the same field that was described in the BASIC DATA 1 screen (see Section 4.2.3). It has been included here for its application to shipping.

REPLACEMENT PART—In this plant-specific field, you can choose whether a material cannot be a replacement part, is an option as a replacement part, or is a mandatory replacement part. This is useful in your engineering control if you are managing discontinued and follow-on parts. For more information on discontinued and follow-on part management, see Chapter 7.

QUALIFY FOR FREE GOODS DISCOUNT—This field is normally only active as a purchasing function, as it applies to receiving a discount when procuring in bulk. For more information on this field, see Section 6.2.1.

MATERIAL FREIGHT GROUP—The material freight group is a locally managed field that is used to calculate freight costs and communicate with forwarding agents. Using the material freight group is also dependent on maintaining your forwarding agent as a vendor, as well as maintenance within the customer master. The material freight group works with the forwarding agent freight group to determine the freight group set, which ultimately determines the freight class. The freight class is a code recognized by those in the transportation industry to classify the means of transportation.

The material freight group also works with the service agent procedure group in the vendor master. This field is used to determine the pricing procedure, which ultimately reads the prices stored in the pricing conditions. By maintaining these fields, you can communicate the cost and means of transportation directly to your forwarding agent.

AVAILABILITY CHECK—The availability check determines how requirements are read and generated in MRP. There are two different ways to maintain the availability check in this locally maintained field, depending on the type of planning you are performing. You can either perform materials planning, which is a standard MRP calculation based upon your dependent and independent requirements. Or, you can perform flexible planning, which is a higher level type of planning that includes MRP elements from the forecast and actual orders when you are maintaining sales and operations planning in SAP.

- ► Materials planning—The choice you make for this field will determine what MRP elements are considered. For instance, purchase orders, reservations, work orders, etc. You will also determine if the check will include all future requirements, or just those within the replenishment period. Finally, you will determine how requirements are generated by stating if requirements can be grouped together, or if they should be generated individually.

- ► Flexible planning—The features of the availability check will work in the same way. However, you must perform further customizing to tie it all together.

APPROVED BATCH RECORD REQUIRED indicator—If you are in a repetitive manufacturing environment, you are most likely using an order type relevant to process orders. For those order types, if you select this indicator, the system will check to see if an approved batch record has been created for your order before performing certain goods movements like a goods receipt or a stock transfer. If a specified batch record has not been created, your movement will not be allowed.

BATCH MANAGEMENT indicator—Depending on your manufacturing environment and costing structure, batch management can have far reaching connections to other components of SAP and can be very difficult to understand for a beginning end user. For instance, if you are in an environment where batches of the same material can be procured externally or produced within your plant, you may wish to activate split valuation with batches. In this case, you are going to valuate your materials individually per batch, which means that batch management is activated for you at the plant level in customizing and cannot be changed by the end user. In another scenario, if you are maintaining configurable materials, you may wish to maintain condition groups within your purchasing information records for each vendor. In this case, you will want to maintain different prices for the same material, from the same vendor, depending upon the material's unique batch configuration.

In simpler environments where valuation is less complex, activating batch management may simply mean that you want to create a batch number for each purchase order or production order that you create. In this type of environment, you are simply looking for inventory control amongst the components of your end products. In some environments, it may be highly critical that each batch of inventory has traceability both to its origin and destination. A good example of this might be a car manufacturer that needs to know the origin and destination of each component within a car for quality assurance purposes. This is an essential element in situations where a recall is necessary.

Managing your inventory in batches lends itself to a multitude of advantageous activities like cycle counting, special stock assignments, financial reporting, and so on.

5.4.2 Shipping data

TRANSPORTATION GROUP—If you are maintaining the necessary elements to automatically calculate shipping routes and costs, the transportation group is an essential component to that calculation.

When processing a delivery against a sales document the system checks for any automatic shipping determinations that you may be maintaining. In order for this to be possible, you must maintain automatic route determinations, shipping condition factors, weights and transportation groups, amongst other things. The transportation group is used to group materials that require similar transportation types. For instance, certain chemicals may require a temperature-controlled shipping environment. Therefore, all chemicals requiring the climate-controlled truck will be part of the same transportation group.

LOADING GROUP—You may want to classify materials by the equipment required to load them into a shipping vessel. For instance, all items that require a 100-ton crane for loading onto a ship may be grouped together. The system uses the loading group in conjunction with the delivery plant and shipping conditions to determine the shipping point. A shipping point is the physical location from which an item may be shipped within a sales organization. For example, if you are using a 100-ton crane to load ships, the shipping point would be the sea freight loading dock.

SETUP TIME—If you are maintaining capacity planning for shipping, you can enter the setup time required to prepare your shipping area for any given material. This field is sales-area dependent and is constant for any quantity of the given material.

PROCESSING TIME—If you are maintaining capacity planning for shipping, you can enter the actual time it takes to process a shipment after the area has been set up. This time is quantity dependent. Therefore, you must maintain a base quantity for capacity planning calculations.

BASE QUANTITY—This is the quantity that applies to your processing time. For example, if your processing time is 10 minutes, your base quantity is 1 pallet, and you have a setup time of 12 minutes, it will take you 62 minutes to load 5 pallets for the planned activities.

Communication with the shipping department is essential

It is wise to include a representative from every functional area during sales and operations planning (S&OP) meetings. The shipping area tends to be a functional group that is overlooked. Some view the shipping activity as a secondary function that does not require much planning. As you have seen in this chapter, shipping, as it relates to sales and distribution, is much more than just putting a box on a truck. It can require intense planning for a complex distribution network. The activities required to complete a shipment can also account for a significant portion of time and cost. It is critical that those controlling the master plan communicate to those in shipping, as well as receive feedback from those individuals. It will be nearly impossible to automate any of the shipping features without a sound mutual understanding of the SAP shipping process.

5.4.3 Packaging material data

MATERIAL GROUP: PACKAGING MATERIALS—A group used to categorize materials by the packaging required for shipment. For example, you can classify all items that require metal banding in one group.

> **Use packaging material groups to assist in government-mandated packing**
>
>  If you are selling items to the U.S. Government, you may be required to follow certain military standard packaging rules. The details of these rules can be very cumbersome and require many different types of packaging for each material. You can use the packaging materials group to aide in planning your packaging material requirements. For example, if you group all items together requiring a particular wooden box, you will be able to get a handle on the amount of wooden boxes that are regularly required.

5.4.4 General plant parameters

NEGATIVE STOCK indicator—By checking this indicator, you are saying that negative stock figures are allowed. You might wonder why anyone would want to do this. Allowing a negative stock value may be useful when the order in which sales are received is important. For instance, you may want to secure a customer order before other customer orders are placed. The inventory will be available in the near future, but no goods receipt has taken place yet.

PROFIT CENTER—By assigning a profit center, you are stating which area of accounting the sale of this product should be settled to and how it is analyzed.

SERIAL NUMBER PROFILE—If you are maintaining product serialization, you must specify the format of your serial numbers. In this field, you will enter the serial number profile, the format of which is defined in SAP customizing.

DISTRIBUTION PROFILE IN PLANT—This field is mostly used when items can go through a complex distribution network, but must arrive to a known recipient.

SERIALIZATION LEVEL—Here you can choose to either make serial numbers unique to the given material only, or all materials. Keep in mind this setting is global, so the setting applies to all plants. It is also important to note that if you want serialization to apply to all materials, you must choose that setting for every material within the organization.

EXTERNAL CUSTOMER REPLENISHMENT PARAMETERS icon—If you are continuously replacing customer stock, for instance, in a pull system, you can maintain the reorder point parameters in the system and view them here.

5.5   Foreign trade export screen

The FOREIGN TRADE EXPORT page (see Figure 5.6) consists of three information sets: FOREIGN TRADE DATA, ORIGIN / EU MARKET ORGANIZATION / PREFERENCES, and LEGAL CONTROL. Unless you are doing large amounts of international trade, it will be unnecessary to maintain most of the fields within this page. Furthermore, if you are buying and selling goods internationally, this page may be maintained by someone such as an import/export control officer. I have included a brief description of each information set below.

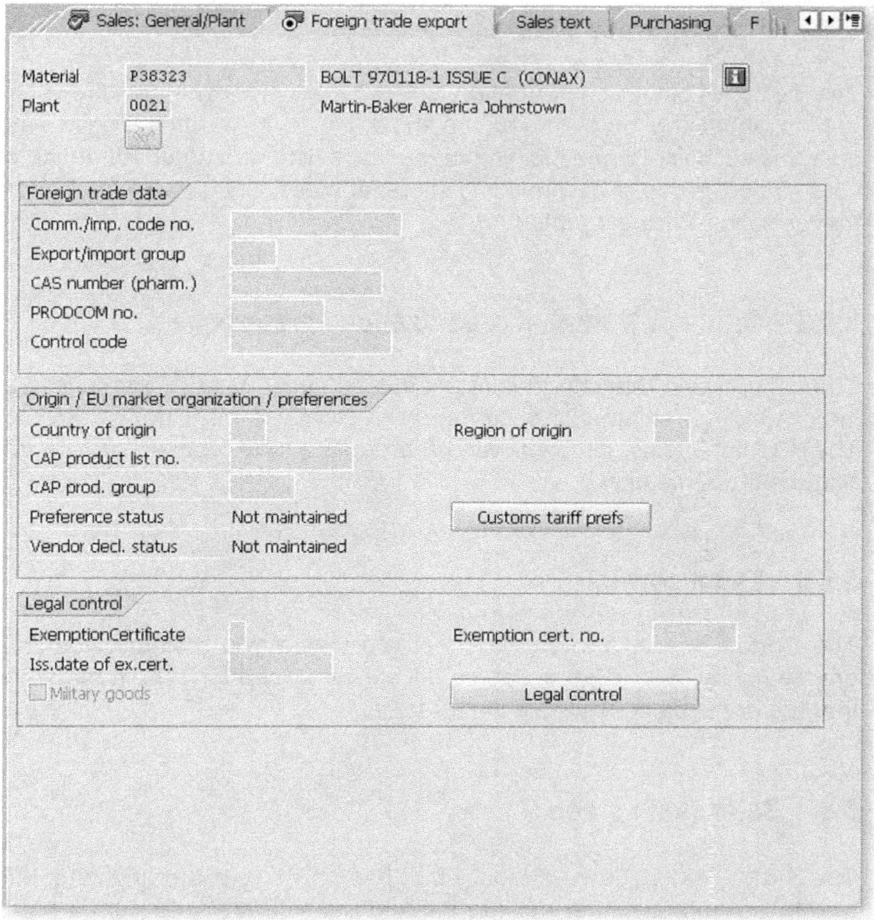

	Sales: General/Plant	Foreign trade export	Sales text	Purchasing	F	◄ ►

Material   P38323   BOLT 970118-1 ISSUE C (CONAX)

Plant   0021   Martin-Baker America Johnstown

Foreign trade data

Comm./imp. code no.

Export/import group

CAS number (pharm.)

PRODCOM no.

Control code

Origin / EU market organization / preferences

Country of origin   Region of origin

CAP product list no.

CAP prod. group

Preference status   Not maintained

Vendor decl. status   Not maintained   [Customs tariff prefs]

Legal control

ExemptionCertificate   Exemption cert. no.

Iss.date of ex.cert.

☐ Military goods   [Legal control]

Figure 5.6: Foreign trade export screen

89

5.5.1 Foreign trade data

The fields within this information set are used to communicate information about the product you are exporting to forwarding agents and customs officials. By maintaining these fields, you can automate much of your import process by providing material classification and tariff information to forwarding agents.

5.5.2 Origin / EU market organization / preferences

The fields within this information set are primarily used to communicate import data for shipments occurring from or within the European Union. The EU maintains its own set of product group codes for the import/export of materials.

5.5.3 Legal control

The fields within this information set are where you maintain your exemption certificates. Exemption certificates are used for certain materials that are not subject to certain import tariffs.

5.6 Sales text screen

The SALES TEXT page (see Figure 5.7) has only one information set. It is simply the text to further explain the material you are selling on a sales order. The text that you enter here will be automatically transferred to each sales order you create. The information stored in the SALES TEXT field is sales-area specific. The text that you insert is only applicable to documents created for your distribution chain. You will still have the ability to amend the text on the sales order itself once you create one.

If you are doing business internationally, you can create sales order texts in different languages. You must first maintain those languages by creating each one by clicking on the CREATE icon within this page. You can only create one sales order text per language.

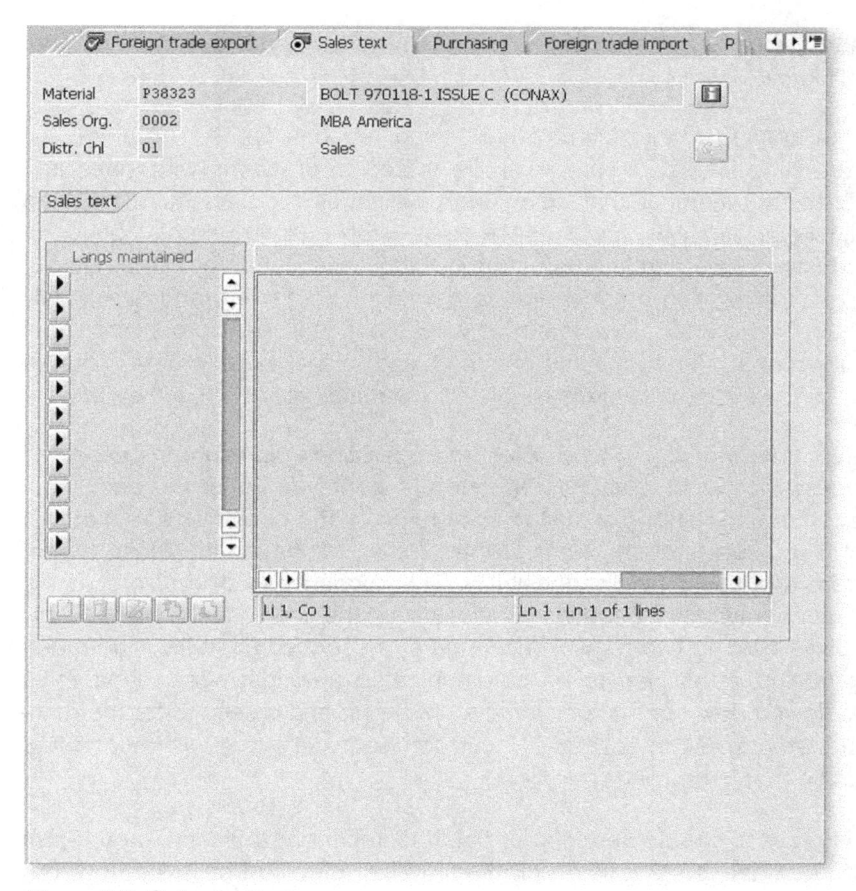

Figure 5.7: Sales text screen

5.7 Personal experience

My personal experience with maintaining the sales area of a material master has been fairly straightforward. The settings available to you in this section are relatively easy to understand, and functions driven by the choices you make in the sales area of the material master are not complex. However, I have found that the incorporation of the sales area screens are often overlooked and mismanaged in some organizations.

During my experiences in consulting for other organizations, I have found that the most frequent problem statement is: "We know what our lead time is, but we can't seem to meet the customer due date and we don't know why!"

There can be many different underlying reasons for this problem, but 99% of the time the reason can be traced to problems with sales and operations planning. Making on-time deliveries requires far more than critical path analysis. As you have seen in this chapter, the distribution of products can be highly automated, but the necessary steps to do so are very complex. You must define, understand, document, and repetitively communicate each component in your order fulfillment process so that all functional areas involved are marching to the same orders. This includes the systematic steps required to manage your ERP software.

I recommend a closed-loop sales and operations planning process. This process involves two steps. One step is identifying all of the necessary procedures in fulfilling a customer order from the customer's request for quote through final shipment of the product, documenting those procedures, and assigning responsibility. The second part of that process is the communication aspect, the closing of the loop, so to speak. This involves holding two regular meetings at prescribed intervals; one meeting for the sales plan to be communicated amongst senior leadership and flowed down to the functional employees, and a second for the functional employees to flow up the current roadblocks that will impede that plan so that it may be reconciled.

This process should be quite formal. It is important to document the process in detail, so that when problems arise, they can be traced back to the fault in the process rather than the usual, ineffective finger pointing that occurs. One of the most important steps in documenting your sales and operations planning process is to include the functions as they relate to your ERP system. This helps to ensure where responsibility for each activity lies, and a very critical aspect of this documentation will be the necessary settings of the sales area within the material master. After all, the settings you choose in this area will help to define how the customer is to receive the product. No sales and operations plan would be complete without describing the final steps necessary to ensure customer satisfaction. I recommend that you research the *Value Stream Analysis* method of identifying and documenting your process. This method will guide you in identifying all steps in your process and include the time it takes to perform each task. When complete, you should be left with an end-to-end process that describes each task, labels the task as value added or non-value added, and assigns a time increment to each activity. This documentation will become the baseline for all future improvement activities, such as removing non-value added tasks and improving process times where possible.

6 Purchasing

In this chapter, I will define the parameters of the material master that control how and when a given material should be procured. The chapter is very specific to the buyer's perspective and offers some great procurement tips.

With the material master (MM) module, you can become a successful buyer by implementing cost-effective procurement strategies, while significantly minimizing repetitive manual effort in purchasing activities. In order to do this, however, you must understand cost effective procurement techniques and the capability and parameters of the system at hand so those strategies can be accurately applied. I wrote this chapter from the buyer's perspective, so that you can understand how your procurement activities are impacted by the material master and, more importantly, to provide a means to effectively control those activities.

In this chapter, we'll cover the essential elements of the SAP procurement process driven by the material master. You will find that your purchasing data components (material information, buyer information, vendor information and legal/foreign trade information) are loosely connected (or not connected at all!) until they are put into focus by the material master. We'll also cover some *best practices* that have proven results in diverse manufacturing environments.

6.1 Purchasing structure in the material master

There are three screens of the material master that pertain directly to purchasing. They are: PURCHASING, FOREIGN TRADE IMPORT, and PURCHASE ORDER TEXT. By selecting the appropriate choices in the fields within these screens, you can assign buyer groups to materials, manage freight classes, manage and automate vendor (purchasing information record) selection, standardize communication with vendors, customize information for purchase orders specific to the material you are buying, and perform a vast array of other purchasing functions. You will find that some fields are managed for your entire global SAP network, while others will be specific to your plant only. These features allow for a geographically diverse purchasing network to communicate and buy commodities efficiently, while customizing unique procurement elements to fit your own facility.

Just like all other sections of the material master, understanding which fields can, should, and must be customized is a key element to success. Another essential element is having a good working relationship with your colleagues who maintain customizing so that your needs can be communicated effectively and implemented in a timely manner.

6.2 Purchasing screen

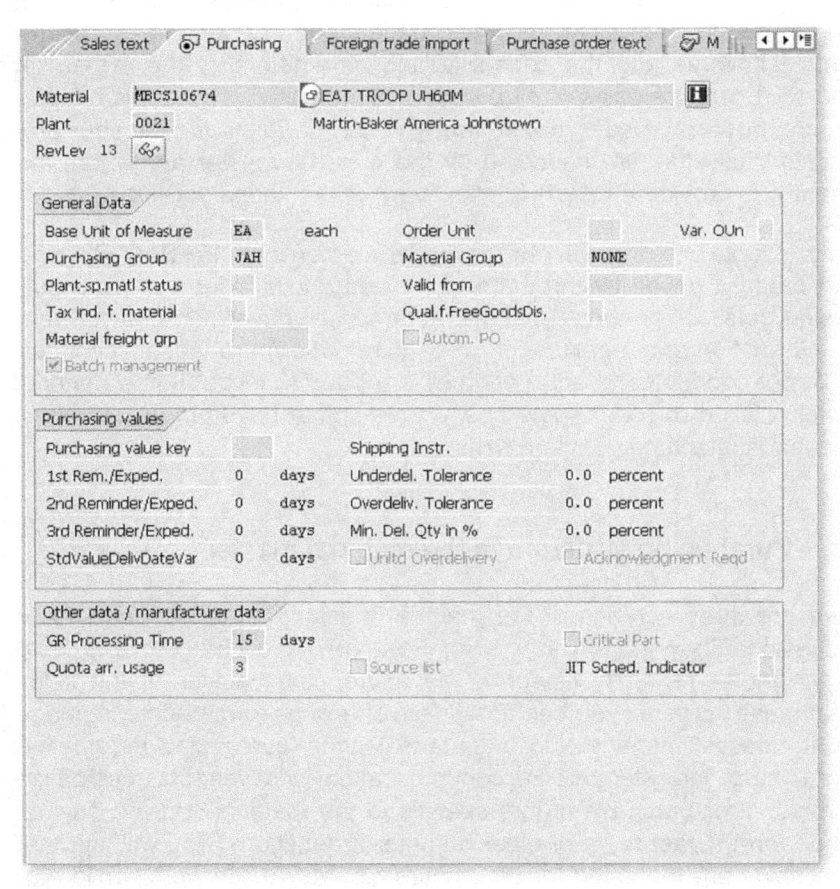

Figure 6.1: Purchasing screen

There are three information sets within the PURCHASING screen (see Figure 6.1): GENERAL DATA, PURCHASING VALUES, and OTHER DATA / MANUFACTURING DATA. The GENERAL DATA information set contains fields that allow you to set special classifications to your material. The PURCHASING VALUES information set contains fields that allow you to customize and automate communication with your vendor. Finally, the OTHER DATA / MANUFACTURING DATA information set contains fields that drive vendor selection and items relevant to delivery scheduling. We'll now explore the fields in each information set and discuss their relationships with each other, as well as their relationship with information stored outside of the material master.

6.2.1 General data

The fields contained in the GENERAL DATA information set are designed to sub-classify your material. By placing further classifications on your material, you can assign buyer responsibility to the material and streamline reporting functions based on the special classifications that you assign to that material. This information set helps to define how a material is handled within your plant.

BASE UNIT OF MEASURE—This is the same field that was previously defined in Chapter 4, but has been included here for reference. The base unit of measure is the overall unit of measure used to manage the stock of a particular material within your organization. A material that is purchased in another unit of measure is converted to the base unit of measure upon goods receipt. This allows for consistency in controlling inventory levels. The base unit of measure is most likely defined by someone who controls the overall stock-keeping unit and it is managed at the global level. It is most likely managed by an IT technician, MRP controller, master scheduler, or inventory control personnel, which means that the decision of what the base unit of measure might be is out of your control. It is the responsibility of the one who decides on the base unit of measure to choose a unit of measure that will define the material in the most precise manner possible, as this unit of measure will be the common denominator to which all alternate units of measure convert to.

ORDER UNIT—As the title of this field suggests, this is the unit of measure for which the item may be ordered and it may differ from the base unit of measure. This field is also globally managed, so it is a good idea to communicate the desired ordering unit to the person who makes this entry.

The unit of measure "Each" (EA) is very commonly used for the base unit of measure because it represents one stock-keeping unit. This allows you to enter a multitude of different order units that will convert to one stock-keeping unit. The relationship between the two units is managed in the conversion factor in the purchasing info record. For instance, in the purchasing information record example below (see Figure 6.2), adhesives are purchased by the case. The unit of measure "Case" (CS) has also been defined as the ORDER UNIT in the material master. One case (CS) of adhesive contains ten units (EA). Therefore, you may order the adhesive by the case, but it can be withdrawn from inventory one unit (EA) at a time.

Purchase Order Unit of Measure					
Order Unit	CS				
Conversion	1	CS	<->	10	EA
Var. Order Unit	Not active				

Figure 6.2: Purchasing info record

Leverage buying power on economies of scale

 This is a great opportunity to use your buying power on economies of scale. If your vendor is going to give you a price reduction for buying items in bulk and your facility has sufficient demand for such a quantity of goods, use the unit of measure conversion factor to ensure that you are buying items in the vendor's recognized unit of measure where the price break occurs.

The base unit of measure and order unit relationship may also assist you in international procurement. For example, you may be buying raw material from Europe in meters (M), but you wish to use the stock keeping unit of feet (FT) in the United States.

VARIABLE PURCHASE ORDER UNIT ACTIVE—If you are part of a large organization, where control over the units of measure resides a great distance from you, you may begin to feel that your buying authority in respect to order unit is out of your control. Don't worry, there is still specific customizing to suit your needs available! By selecting 'Active' in the VARIABLE PURCHASE ORDER UNIT field, you can choose a unit of measure on the purchase order that differs from the unit of measure in the purchasing info record. Be careful, this field is also managed globally. Make sure that it is part of your corporate strategy to allow for this field to be activated because it will also be active for all other purchasing organizations within your company once it is selected for the material in question. I've found this helpful when purchasing commercial off-the-shelf (COTS) items that can vary in container size from time to time. For example, I use a small local shop to purchase a lubricant. That shop will buy bulk amounts of lubricant from China whenever a discounted price is offered. However, the discounted price can apply to different container sizes depending on what the Chinese supplier wants to liquidate. So, one week I may be buying by the kilogram and other weeks I may be buying by the drum.

PURCHASING GROUP—In this field, you will choose the purchasing group code that you are a part of as a buyer. This code may pertain to you as an individual, or the group of buyers that you are part of. By maintaining this field, buyers can view purchasing data reports that pertain to the materials for which they are responsible. This field will also automate communication to your vendors by applying your purchasing group information to SAP-generated communications involving the materials to which your purchasing group has been assigned. The choices made available to you in this field are created in SAP customizing. If you wish to amend the choices available in this field, you must contact the individual responsible for customizing.

> ## Create accountability by assigning an individual buyer
>
>  The field PURCHASING GROUP is best utilized by assigning a material to an individual, not a group of individuals. This way, responsibilities are clearly defined to one person. That buyer can easily view and process requisitions and purchase orders that are assigned to them in their requisition and purchase order reports. The alternative is to assign a few people to one buyer group. This results in more manual effort because the group must decide how to split up their work load without the automation of SAP. This can create the potential for unprocessed requisitions and delays in precious manufacturing time. As you will see Figure 6.3, we've used the buyer's initials as the buyer group code. Now she, along with everyone else in the organization, knows who is responsible for procuring this material.

General Data					
Base Unit of Measure	EA	each	Order Unit		Var. OUn
Purchasing Group	JAH		Material Group	NONE	
Plant-sp.matl status			Valid from		
Tax ind. f. material			Qual.f.FreeGoodsDis.		
Material freight grp			☐ Autom. PO		
☑ Batch management					

Figure 6.3: General data—buyer group

MATERIAL GROUP—Again, this field was defined in Chapter 4, but is being included here due to its relevance to purchasing. This field is used to group classes of material together that share similar characteristics. It may not be necessary to maintain this field if you are a business that is not diverse in its product structure or a business that does not maintain many stock keeping units. The benefit of this field is that it allows you to refine the scope of your reports to specific types of materials for analysis by reporting on only the material group that you are interested in. The choices in this field are also predetermined for you in SAP customizing. To use this field effectively, a material group hierarchy must be created to maintain each group. This field is maintained globally. You might find this field useful when buying raw materials. For example, if you are grouping metal by type, you can analyze the amount of aluminum purchased versus steel to see where you should focus on cost reduction techniques.

PLANT SPECIFIC MATERIAL STATUS – As opposed to the previous fields we've discussed, which are maintained globally, this field is intended specifically for you to restrict the usage of a given material in your particular plant. You will find unlimited inventory control potential in this field. You can restrict material transactions regarding materials management, production planning, plant maintenance, warehouse management, and costing. There will be several choices available that are installed from the start of your SAP implementation. The selection choice "block for procurement," for example, may be available. However, the most effective choices made available to you in this field are created in SAP customizing and can be very specific to your plant's needs. By making entries in this field, you can have SAP generate warning or error messages during certain functions pertaining to this material. If you, or someone else responsible for this material, for instance a material planner, wish to restrict the usage of a certain material, you must inform the person who manages the customizing of this material in SAP of your desired rule. He or she will then make it available as a selection choice to you in the material master.

Case example: Plant-specific material status

 Janet R. is a buyer for a women's clothing retailer. She has been receiving complaints from her sales representative that the stitching in lady's undergarments has been fraying and that immediate action must be taken or sales will decline significantly. Janet approaches her quality control department about the problem, but is told that although they acknowledge that some aesthetic defects have been noticed, the garments have consistently met the specifications and quality standards written in the inspection profile. Janet's sales rep tells her that she must find another way to stop these defective products from reaching the customer at any cost. Janet is aware of her inventory control power in SAP. She contacts her IT department and asks them to create a new plant-specific material status choice. The plant-specific material status that is created will now generate an error message upon each receipt of the material to which it is applied.

This error message will prevent an automatic goods receipt into inventory and will be shown to the person performing the goods receipt in the form of a pop-up error message on their SAP screen. It will state: "Do not post to inventory. Send all items to Janet R. for evaluation." Janet has ensured personal control over the situation at hand with no further systematic effort required.

VALID FROM—This field is also locally controlled and works in conjunction with the plant-specific material status. If you choose not to maintain a date in this field, the choice you have made in the plant-specific material status field will remain active indefinitely, until it is either changed or removed. However, applying a validity date can be very useful in planning for any given unique situation.

To use this field effectively, one must understand how MRP recognizes a valid-from date. The plant-specific material status that you choose will only be valid on a purchase order that has a planning date after the valid-from date. If you set a valid-from date as June 1, any purchase order that you create after June 1 will recognize the intended plant-specific material status. If you create a purchase order on May 28, the status is ignored and no special status is applied. The valid-from date may be set to any date, but for practical purposes SAP checks your entry against the current date. If you enter a date that is in the past, depending upon your settings in customizing, you are either presented with a warning or error message to that effect.

Case example: Plant-specific material status with validity date

Sanjay is a buyer for a bicycle manufacturer. He is responsible for releasing cost estimates for his company on a monthly basis. He is told that beginning August 1st, the front brake lever, which is part of a BOM structure for an entire bicycle, will change material numbers. The material number will change from LEVER691 to LEVERFRNT. Sanjay will have to release several cost estimates before August 1st, using the existing material number LEVER691, but he wants to ensure that it is not part of a cost estimate after the cut-in date of the new part.

Sanjay finds that he has a plant-specific material status of "cancelled part" as an available choice in the material master, which issues an error message during cost estimating once it is applied. To coincide with the cut-in date of the new material number, Sanjay installs the valid-from date of August 1st for the plant-specific material status of LEVER691. This error will now appear on any cost estimate for bicycles containing LEVER691 after August 1st and the cost estimate cannot be released.

TAX INDICATOR FOR MATERIAL (PURCHASING)—This field is locally controlled. It allows you to automatically assign a tax code to a material for the purpose of purchasing. It may be useful if you are trying to apply tax rules to different types of inventory. For instance, you may wish to apply a different tax code to a material that is placed into stock than a material that is immediately consumed. Automatic tax determination can be useful. However, SAP will override any entry made in this field of the material master if tax determination data is maintained in customizing or in the pricing conditions maintained in the vendor master. Furthermore, the tax information functionality is far better when accurately controlled in the vendor master.

QUALIFY FOR FREE GOODS DISCOUNT (PURCHASING)—This field is maintained globally. Therefore, the decision to obtain a discount will apply to the material master for your entire organization. However, this does not mean that if you select to obtain a discount that all other plants in your organization will also receive discounts automatically when procuring this item. You must also make the selection to receive a discount in your vendor master. Furthermore, you must create a link between the vendor, material, plant, and the purchase organization in the form of a purchasing condition, making the discount unique to your purchasing activities only. Finally, some work in customizing must be done to define the rules of your discounts. There are two types of what SAP refers to as "discount in kind" for purchasing and they are described below.

▶ Inclusive discount in kind—This type of discount means that the discounted quantity is included within the base quantity of the order. For instance, if a buyer creates a purchase order for 10,000 units and the vendor has agreed that you will receive an additional 1,000 units free of charge for every 5,000 units ordered, the buyer will only pay for 8,000 units, but the quantity will be 10,000 units on the purchase order.

▶ Exclusive discount in kind—Conversely, this type of discount means that the discounted quantity is over and above the base quantity of the order. In this instance, if a buyer places a purchase order for 10,000 units, and the vendor agrees to provide 1,000 units free of charge for every 5,000 units ordered, the buyer will pay for 10,000 units, but receive 12,000 units on that purchase order.

Much of what I have described here is beyond the scope of this text in regard to vendor master setup and customizing. However, discount in kind purchasing is a very useful cost saving measure when it is implemented appropriately. It is most useful in wholesale and distribution companies that buy and sell large amounts of commodities, where additional goods are supplied free of charge when large purchases are made.

MATERIAL FREIGHT GROUP—The material freight group is a locally managed field that is used to calculate freight costs and communicate with shipping agents. Like discounts in kind, using the material freight group is also dependent on maintenance within the vendor master. The material freight group works with the forwarding agent freight group to determine the freight group set, which ultimately determines the freight class. The freight class is a code recognized by those in the transportation industry to classify the means of transportation.

The material freight group also works with the service agent procedure group in the vendor master. This field is used to determine the pricing procedure, which ultimately reads the prices stored in the pricing conditions. By maintaining these fields, you can communicate the cost and means of transportation directly to your forwarding agent. You can also report on materials that ship by certain means of transportation. For example, you could look at all materials that ship by rail if you've maintained the material freight group field that way.

AUTOMATIC PURCHASE ORDER indicator—By activating this feature, you can automate the creation of a purchase order once the requisition reaches its planned creation date in MRP. The automation can be so highly functional that, if communication methods are properly defined in the vendor master, a purchase order can be created and sent to the vendor without any further action by the buyer.

This field is maintained locally in the material master. However, it does not function unless the AUTOMATIC PURCHASE ORDER indicator is flagged in the vendor master as well. Vendor master data is universal information for all plants within the organization, so many fields are maintained globally. This means that it must be part of your corporate strategy to automatically release purchase orders before you can proceed.

This function is highly recommended for recurring purchases, particularly with vendors with whom you have long-term (schedule or contract) agreements and/or quota arrangements with your company. It's a wonderful tool to reduce purchase order processing time and ultimately the material lead time. The important part is to have all of the data you wish to communicate set up accurately and in advance, as you will not have an opportunity to adjust information on each purchase order as it is sent.

Lean manufacturing opportunity

 If you are implementing lean manufacturing techniques and are looking to reduce waste in the value chain, manual purchase order creation is, as lean practitioners will say, "low-hanging fruit." Automatic purchase order creation is a simple tool to reduce overall lead time and cost (purchase order processing fee) in the supply chain. Many businesses undertaking a lean initiative are transitioning planning and procurement functions into one planner/buyer role. This consolidation of efforts allows someone in a planning role to streamline the manufacturing process by using their intimate knowledge of manufacturing requirements and translating that information into precision procurement. Activating automatic purchase orders is a significant help to an individual who now has many responsibilities within the organization.

BATCH MANAGEMENT—This is the same field that was discussed in Chapter 5. For the purposes of this chapter, the important thing to take away is the fact that the batch management indicator must be selected to manage your inventory in batches. If the choice is up to you, you may choose not to manage some material in batches on occasion. For instance, if you are buying general hand tools for plant maintenance, it may not be necessary or practical to manage those items in batches. For more information on batch management and valuation, see Chapter 5 and Chapter 10.

6.2.2 Purchasing values

PURCHASING VALUE KEY—This is a wonderful tool to automate communication with your vendor after your purchase order or request for quotation has been sent. It allows for automatic reminders to be sent to your vendor at specified intervals, both before the order or quotation is due, or as a reminder that either the order or quotation is late. The field is maintained globally and may come with several standard selections made available by SAP. However, the tolerances of each reminder and the other seven parameters are easily maintained in customizing, so a purchasing value key tailored to suit your particular needs is very simply created by your customizer. It is important to know that if you maintain communication data, such as reminders, in your purchasing information record, that data supersedes the purchasing value key data stored in the material master.

> ▶ Reminders—You can set up to three reminders to send to your vendor. The reminder feature is keyed off of the delivery date of the purchase order or due date of the quotation. If you maintain several reminders, they must be in ascending order and for a continuous range. For example: Reminder 1—(15 days before order due date), Reminder 2—(10 days before order due date), and Reminder 3—(5 days before order due date). Reminders can be sent to the vendor prior to the due date by using a negative number or after the due date by using a positive number.

> ▶ Shipping instruction—Simply an instruction that you can apply to your reminder communication. The instruction you wish to convey must be defined in customizing.

> ▶ Delivery tolerances—You can define the amount of over delivery, under delivery, and minimum acceptable delivery all by the percentage of the order quantity. The values maintained in the material master are suggested to you when you create a purchasing information record for that material. If no purchasing information record exists, the material master values are applied to any purchase order that you create. By selecting the UNLIM-

ITED OVER DELIVERY indicator, you are granting your vendor authority to deliver over and above the original order quantity with no restrictions.

- ▶ Acknowledgement required—If this field is selected, it simply applies a statement to your reminders to the vendor that an acknowledgement of the reminder is required.

- ▶ Standardizing value for delivery date variance—This parameter is used to determine how many days are to be considered as variance from the due date of your purchase order These statistics are used in calculating vendor ratings.

Reminders can be wasteful

 Do not send reminders prior to the purchase order or quotation due date to vendors that are consistently performing satisfactorily and with whom you have a strong relationship. These documents will simply become routine annoyances that will get deleted by the vendor. Therefore, when an actual concern arises, the automatic feature will not be effective. The purchasing value key is very effective when bringing on new suppliers, as it will enforce your insistence on timely delivery performance.

6.2.3 Other data / manufacturing data

GOODS RECEIPT PROCESSING TIME—This field is maintained locally because it pertains to the lead time within your plant. It is used in MRP to account for the time after the item is received, up until the time it is placed into stock. It should account for all activity times (in days) required to process the receipt, inspection, and storage of the material. Unless you are in a sophisticated logistics environment, where goods receipts occur with advanced technology like radio frequency identification (RFID) that is used to trigger dock-to-stock receiving and storage transactions, it is necessary that you maintain this field. Otherwise, MRP will not account for the internal lead time of a purchased material.

CRITICAL PART—This field is maintained locally because it applies to your plant's inventory sampling procedure. That is, if you select for this field to be active, 100% of the inventory of this material will be considered a "must count" in your physical inventory count (cycle count) process. It may also be useful to you for table reporting purposes if you wish to designate certain materials that should receive additional attention of some kind.

QUOTA ARRANGEMENT USAGE—This field is maintained locally, as it applies to the supply from procurement and production within your plant. It is used to determine which business processes are included in your quota arrangement. The choices for business processes include purchase orders, purchase requisitions, schedule agreements, planned orders, MRP, and production orders. The choice you make here determines how the total order quantity is calculated in the quota arrangement, thereby determining which source of supply is used for a material at a particular point in time.

Note: Mixed procurement type requires special setting

To include supply by both in-house production and external procurement for a given material, you must select the procurement type (X—both procurement types) in the PROCUREMENT TYPE field of the MRP 2 screen.

If you are not familiar with quota arrangements, they are a wonderful tool to automatically split workloads among several suppliers, and even in-house production, by percentage for a valid period of time.

Case example: Quota arrangement

Michael works as a buyer for a small business that makes custom furniture with annual sales of $3M. His shop has historically made all of his knobs, hinges, and other metal fittings in-house. Due to a recent industrial boom in the technology sector, the population in Michael's region has been growing exponentially for the past year. This boom has brought in a number of high-earning professionals with an appetite for custom-made furniture.

Due to this increase in demand, Michael's forecasted sales for the coming year are now $7M. He now needs to rethink his method of component supply, as his manufacturing shop does not have the capacity to produce the required amount of metal fittings. Furthermore, none of the local metal fabrication shops have the capacity to handle this demand alone. To solve this problem, Michael calls a conference of three local machine shops, along with his production manager. He explains the dilemma and the sales potential to each party. Each party expresses their available capacity for this project to Michael, who then translates those figures into a percentage of the total demand. These percentages are incorporated into a quota arrangement for a set period of time. With the quota arrangement in place, MRP will now automate who will receive an order at a given point in time within the quota arrangements validity period.

SOURCE LIST—This field is maintained locally, as it pertains to the list of vendors available to supply your plant a given material during a given validity period. By selecting this indicator, you are stating that a source list must be maintained in order to place a purchase order. If you are consistently using a sole supplier for a material, maintaining a source list is unnecessary.

In the source list you can select the vendor you want to use at that point in time by choosing "fixed source." You may also temporarily block vendors from use in the source list. The vendor that you choose as the fixed source will be the vendor tied to planned orders and requisitions created by MRP.

If you are creating a quota arrangement for a material, you must maintain a source list that contains the vendors you are applying to the quota arrangement. You must also maintain a source list if you are going to use schedule agreements with your vendors. The link between what sources are included in MRP scheduling, quota arrangements, and scheduling agreements are maintained in the source list. The source list is the vendor selection master, if you will.

In the following source list example (see Figure 6.4), you will see that the buyer has selected two vendors relevant to MRP scheduling. Those vendors also happen to be enrolled in a schedule agreement for this material. The other vendors stored in the source list may be used at any time. However, they must be selected manually during purchase order creation.

⊞ Display Source List: Overview Screen

🗗 🔍

Material	MBCS13080	FRAME LOWER SIDE RH
Plant	0021	Martin-Baker America Johnstown

Source List Records

Valid from	Valid to	Vendor	POrg	PPl	OUn	Agmt	Item	Fix	Blk	MRP	MRP Area
01/01/1989	12/31/2099	21029	0002				0				
01/01/1989	12/31/2099	21110	0002				0				
01/01/1989	12/31/2099	21013	0002				0				
01/01/1989	12/31/2099	21163	0002				0				
01/01/1989	12/31/2099	21194	0002				0				
01/01/1989	12/31/2099	21200	0002				0				
01/01/2013	03/31/2014	21029	0002		EA	4600000065	30		1		0021
01/01/2013	03/31/2014	21013	0002		EA	4600000069	20		1		0021

Figure 6.4: Source list

To allow the two preferred sources (vendors 21029 and 21013) to share the demand requirements, we have set the quota arrangement usage to "3" in the PURCHASING screen of the material master (see Figure 6.5). This selection is configured to consider purchase orders, purchase requisitions, schedule agreements, planned orders, and material requirements planning (MRP) in the total order calculation. It is not configured to consider production orders, as this material is not made in-house.

Other data / manufacturer data				
GR Processing Time	15	days		☐ Critical Part
Quota arr. usage	3		☐ Source list	JIT Sched. Indicator

Figure 6.5: Other data / manufacturing data—Quota arrangement usage

Furthermore, if you see the quota arrangement for this material below (see Figure 6.6), you will find that the total order quantity will be split 50% / 50% between the two vendors. You can also see that any given order must be in a minimum quantity of at least 100 units before an individual order will be split between the two suppliers (minimum quantity field). If the order quantity is less than 100 units, the normal quota arrangement rules will apply. You now have an MRP environment where orders are automatically split between two preferred vendors per your specifications, none of which is possible without maintaining the source list.

Display Quota Arrangement: Overview of Quota Arr. Items 850

👤 Header ▶ Next Overview

Material	MBCS13080	⎘ AME LOWER SIDE RH
Plant	0021	Martin-Baker America Johnstown
Quota Arr.	850	Base Unit	EA
Valid from	02/01/2013	Valid to	03/31/2014
		Minimum Qty	100.000
Created by	JHALL	Created on	01/29/2013

Quota Arr. Items

QAI	P	S	Vendor	PPl	PVer	Qu.	in %	Allocated Qty	Maximum Quantity	Quota Base Qty
1	F		21029			50	50.0	163.000	0.000	0.000
2	F		21013			50	50.0	140.000	0.000	0.000

Figure 6.6: Quota arrangement

JIT SCHEDULE indicator—This field is maintained locally. By activating this indicator you can generate just-in-time delivery schedules for a schedule agreement. Just-in-time delivery schedules can provide your vendor with the exact quantity and delivery date required in respect to near-term requirements.

The use of just-in-time scheduling requires that you and your vendor are engaged in a very close working relationship where there is a mutual understanding that you are operating in a lean environment. In this situation, your vendor is set up to respond immediately to your demands under specified parameters.

6.3 Foreign trade import screen

The FOREIGN TRADE IMPORT screen (see Figure 6.7) consists of three information sets: FOREIGN TRADE DATA, ORIGIN / EU MARKET ORGANIZATION / PREFERENCES, and LEGAL CONTROL. Unless you are doing large amounts of international trade, it will be unnecessary to maintain most of the fields within this screen. Furthermore, if you are buying and selling goods internationally, this screen may be maintained by someone such as an import/export control officer. A brief description of each information set is listed below.

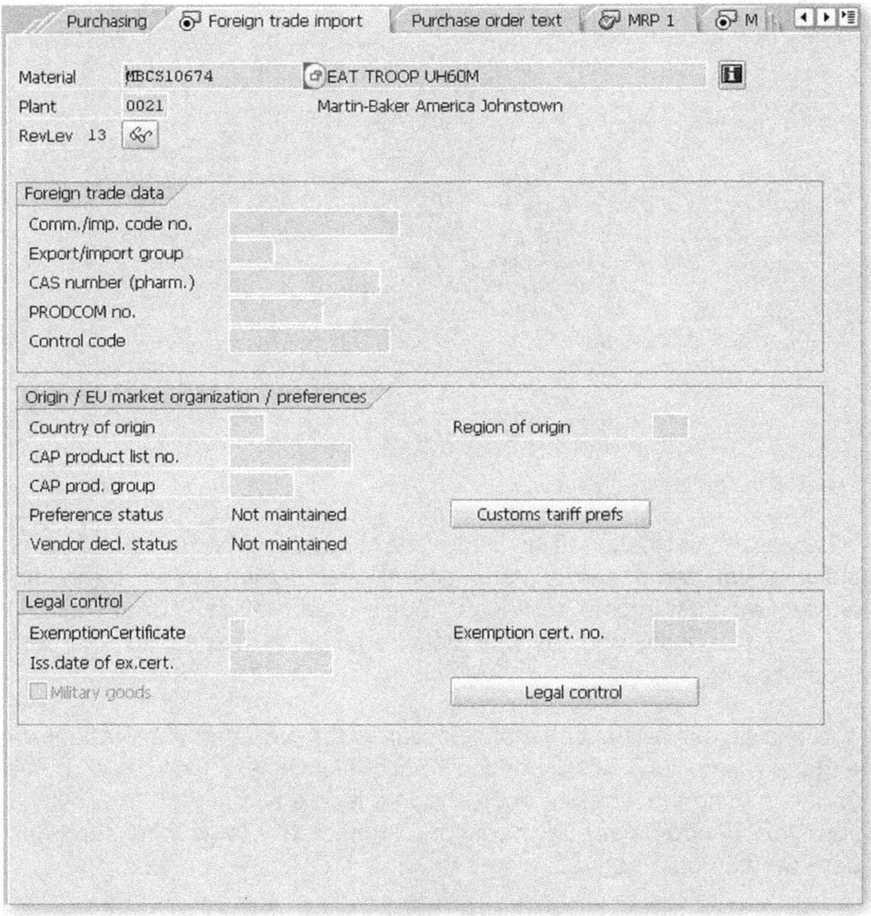

Figure 6.7: Foreign trade import screen

6.3.1 Foreign trade data

The fields within this information set are used to communicate information about the product you are importing to forwarding agents and customs officials. By maintaining these fields, you can automate much of your import process by providing material classification and tariff information to forwarding agents.

6.3.2 Origin / EU market organization / preferences

The fields within this information set are primarily used to communicate import data for shipments occurring from or within the European Union (EU). The EU maintains its own set of product group codes for the import and export of materials.

6.3.3 Legal control

The fields within this information set are where you maintain exemption certificates. Exemption certificates are used for materials that are not subject to certain import tariffs.

6.4 Purchase order text screen

The PURCHASE ORDER TEXT screen (see Figure 6.8) only has one information set. It is simply the text to further explain the material you are ordering on a purchase order. The text you enter here will be automatically transferred to each purchase order you create. The information stored in the purchase order text field is global. So the text that you apply should not be particular to your plant. If you need to apply local control, you will still have the ability to amend the text on the purchase order itself once you create one.

If you are doing business internationally, you can create purchase order texts in different languages. You must first maintain those languages by creating each one by clicking on the CREATE icon within this screen. You can only create one purchase order text per language.

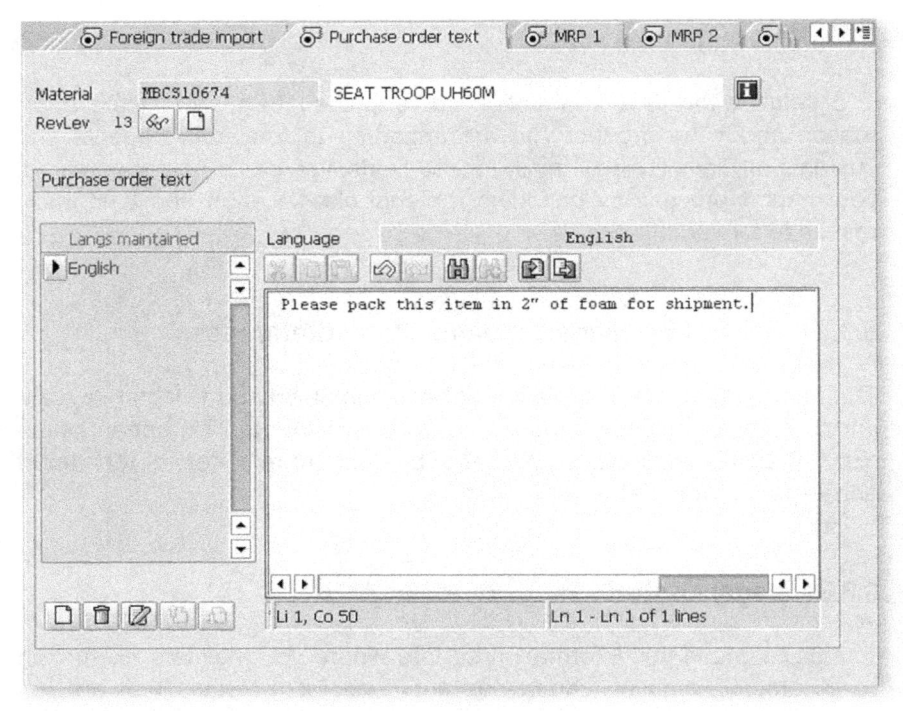

Figure 6.8: Purchase order text screen

6.5 Personal experience

Early in my manufacturing career as a production planner, I was fortunate enough to work very closely with the buyer for my product line. We worked together prior to our SAP implementation and we were lucky enough to grow together (and unfortunately, sometimes apart) in our material master education as SAP became our ERP system. Together, we've experienced several conflicts, obstacles, and setbacks in our planning and procurement roles. This was not because we were working against one another, but because we had different perspectives on how the material master handled our data, who was responsible for certain activities, and how to communicate and coordinate those activities with one another.

We were able to find our path to effective communication and efficiency in materials management in two ways. First, we developed an open line of constant communication and trust. Second, we began to educate one another on the functions and fields of the material master as we learned them, since we had common terminology by which to communicate those functions.

SAP is a wonderful tool for automation and control, but it is not a substitute for human interaction and teamwork. Here is an example of one of the issues that we experienced, and I hope that as a buyer, this will help you to overcome similar obstacles.

As a buyer, you will maintain a lead time in each purchasing information record you create. If you are new to the SAP Material Master, you may assume that the data within the purchasing information record that you choose as your current source will drive MRP lead time data. As we now know, this is not correct. It is, in fact, the lead time stored in the PLANNED DELIVERY TIME field of the MRP 2 screen that drives MRP lead time data.

We would find ourselves making several fatal errors. For one, we would set the planned delivery time to match the lead time of the very first vendor we purchased material from. Let's say it was sixty (60) days. As time went on, other vendors would be selected as the source for the given material. Those new sources would have much longer lead times in some cases, perhaps one hundred (100) days. The buyer would assume that by creating a new purchasing info record with an accurate lead time and selecting that vendor as the source that the lead time would automatically drive MRP. After several breakdowns in the supply chain, we realized our error. Of course, the planned delivery time was still set at sixty (60) days. Therefore, our requisitions were now being released forty (40) days too late!

Secondly, now that we knew that the planned delivery time must be updated to match the current lead time, we weren't sure how to communicate that data, or whose responsibility it was to update it. After several interdepartmental discussions, we found it best for our organization that the buyer should update the PLANNED DELIVERY TIME field in MRP 2 as new vendors were selected as the preferred source, then communicate this activity to the materials planner via e-mail for their information.

The moral of this story is that in any given organization there will most likely be several end users from diverse business functions entering and relying on material master data. You must communicate with and learn to trust those individuals to run materials management effectively. It behooves you to educate one another as much as possible, to draw clear lines of responsibility within the material master, and develop formal internal documented processes and procedures to account for it all.

Note: Retail version differs from manufacturing

 An important piece of information to take away from this segment is that in a make-to-order environment, someone is responsible for the manual maintenance of the PLANNED DELIVERY TIME field. However, in a retail setting, that time can be suggested for you by the range of your vendor masters.

7 Planning

I believe this chapter is one of the most important to your understanding of the material master. In this chapter, I will define how requirements are planned through the settings that you make in the SAP Material Master, and how production activities are scheduled to meet those requirements.

I have said before that the heart of materials management in SAP lies in the material master. To take that statement one step further, at the center of the material master is requirements planning. The elements of requirements planning are what tie together all other functions of the material master into a production system. The settings you make within the screens described in this chapter are critical to interpreting the inputs of sales and transitioning those requirements into achievable actions as driven by MRP. Those who maintain the following screens will have the greatest impact on shop floor control, procurement scheduling, inventory levels, requirements consumption, and capacity management, just to name a few critical tasks involved in running daily operations.

This chapter is particularly special to me, as I have spent the majority of my career working in this segment of operations. It has taken years of mentoring, practice, education, and mistakes to gain a solid understanding of the inner workings of MRP within SAP. Because this segment of the material master can have such an impact on so many aspects of the business, your understanding of the settings must be sound. Furthermore, your understanding of planning theory must also be concrete before you can effectively apply these settings.

In this chapter, I'll cover the essential SAP Material Master elements that you have at your disposal to become a great materials planner. However, in order to do so, it is also critical that you are communicating with other functional areas that your MRP settings will impact, as those settings will greatly affect how those individuals will conduct business and process their own SAP transactions.

It should be noted that because the material master offers so many options, there are several different possible approaches to address the same issue. It is your responsibility to choose the approach that has the necessary functionality to suits your needs, while also invoking the least amount of unwanted, additional functionality that may hinder performance.

Finally, you will find that I've added a bonus section in this chapter to describe the subcontracting process. This is a process I've recently learned to use to supply raw materials to suppliers in need. I find it to be very effective in reducing lead times and negotiating procurement prices.

7.1 Planning structure in the material master

There are six material master screens that apply to planning. They are: MRP 1, MRP 2, MRP 3, MRP 4, FORECASTING, and WORK SCHEDULING. The selections that you make in the fields on these screens will govern how planned orders are generated, define the make/buy decision, determine material lead times, regulate the consumption of requirements, and facilitate many, many more standard planning functions. Finally, in this section of the material master is where the planner is assigned responsibility for a material, which can be a critical piece of information in the material master for when shop floor control questions arise.

Many of the fields within this section of the material master are plant-specific, as similar activities can vary in structure and process from plant to plant in any given organization. Therefore, you will have the ability to run your plant according to the internal and external factors that may influence your particular facility.

7.2 MRP 1 screen

There are four information sets within the MRP 1 screen (see Figure 7.1). They are: GENERAL DATA, MRP PROCEDURE, LOT SIZE DATA, and MRP AREAS. The general data information set contains basic information that a planner may want to know about a material. The MRP procedure information set contains information on the method of planning that applies to a material. The lot size data is information that will control the frequency and size of your planned orders, which will ultimately become your purchase and production orders. The MRP area's information set is used when you are maintaining separate and special MRP planning parameters for the selected material.

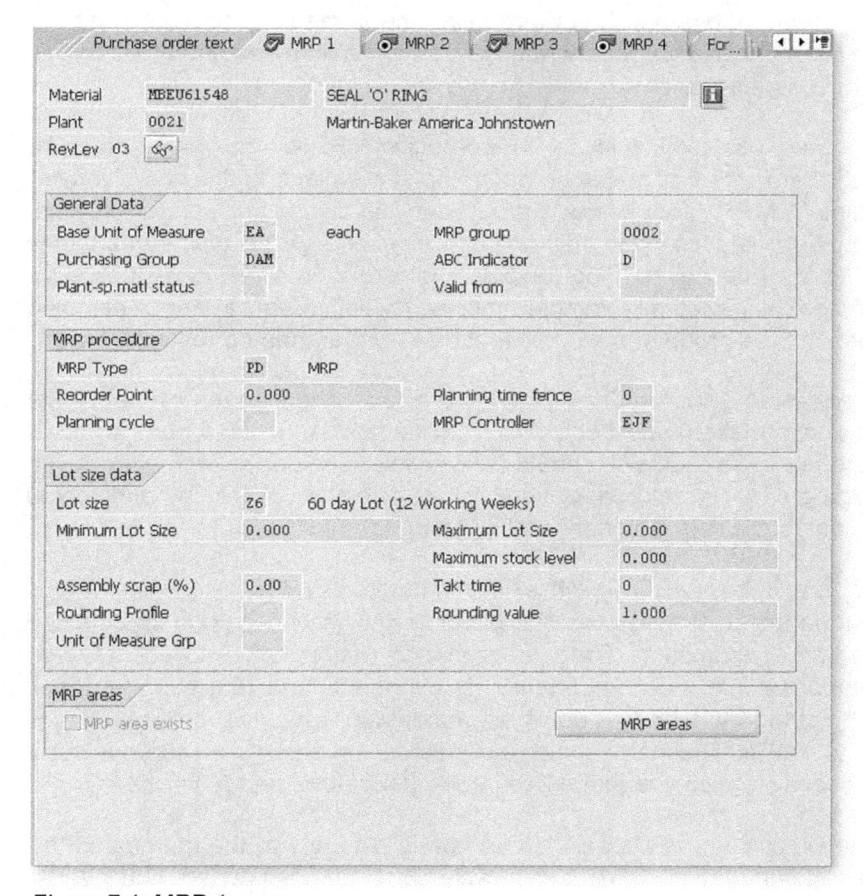

Figure 7.1: MRP 1 screen

7.2.1 General data

BASE UNIT OF MEASURE—This is the same field that was defined in Chapter 4. For more information, see Section 4.2.1. I have incorporated it into this screen for reference.

MRP GROUP—The total planning calculation that will be set to run automatically at a specified interval in SAP customizing will control your overall MRP activity. It will contain the planning strategy for your plant, as well as specific parameters that govern how requirements are consumed and grouped together. If you are using the same parameters for the entire plant, those parameters may be differentiated by material type only in SAP customizing.

However, you may want to have specific MRP control parameters for particular groups of materials within the same plant. In this case, you will maintain MRP groups. Each group can have different control parameters. For instance, you may wish to plan one group of materials in a make-to-order environment and another group in a make-to-stock environment. As another example, you may want to use a longer planning horizon for a group of materials that have longer than normal lead times.

PURCHASING GROUP—This field was previously defined in Chapter 6. For more information, see Section 6.2.1. This field is included here for reference. As a planner, you should be working very closely with your buyer. If you are in a large organization with many buyers, this field will help you to contact the relevant individual or group.

ABC indicator—ABC analysis is a method of classifying materials by importance. In some cases, the factor of importance is price. In others, it may be consumption. The idea is that all materials fit into one of three categories: (A) most important, (B) important, and (C) less important. Each category is broken down by percentage, which will collectively add up to 100%. The percentage you choose for each is up to you, but a normal distribution might be (A) = 20%, (B) = 30%, and (C) = 50%.

You will assign the chosen ABC analysis category to the material in this field. It is a critical element to a cycle count process, where you want to arrange the frequency in which each material is counted in inventory by its importance to the organization.

PLANT SPECIFIC MATERIAL STATUS—This field was also previously defined in Chapter 6. For more information, see Section 6.2.1. The field is included here because planners, as well as buyers, may have cause to implement a material restriction.

VALID FROM—This field was also previously defined in Chapter 6. For more information, see Section 6.2.1.

7.2.2 MRP procedure

MRP TYPE—The selection you make in this plant-specific field will determine the method that is used to plan your material. I will describe the standard choices, but there are more possibilities available, like master production scheduling, time-phased planning, and vendor managed inventory planning. In most cases, the following standard choices will cover your needs.

- ▶ ND—No planning. In this case, no planning takes place for the selected material during the MRP run. This may be useful for discontinued parts that you want to keep a record of, but do not want to procure or produce.

- ▶ PD—MRP planning. This choice will make the material subject to the planning parameters that have been defined in your standard MRP planning run, or the specific parameters that have been assigned to the MRP group to which the selected material belongs. This is the standard choice for valued materials that are produced and procured in a normal production environment.

- ▶ VB—Manual reorder point planning. By selecting reorder point planning, you are telling the system not to apply the MRP planning run to the selected material. Instead, you are telling the system to replenish stock only when the inventory level drops below a certain value, which is defined in the following field, REORDER POINT. In the case of manual reorder points, you must personally calculate the reorder point and insert that value in the REORDER POINT field. With this selection, sales order and dependent requirement quantities are not deducted from the inventory quantity. Reorder points can be easily calculated by the following formula:

Reorder point = Average demand per day x Lead time in days + Safety stock

- ▶ VM—Automatic reorder point planning. This choice can be selected if you are using forecast planning. In this case, the reorder point is calculated for you automatically and inserted into the reorder point field. The system uses historical values and updates the reorder point field during each specified forecast calculation period. With this selection, the system will not include current sales orders and dependent requirements in the calculation.

- ▶ V1—Manual reorder point planning including external requirements. This selection requires you to calculate and enter your own reorder point. However, in this case, sales order and dependent requirement quantities are seen as a deduction from inventory by the system.

- ▶ V2—Automatic reorder point with external requirements. This is the same calculation that is performed with MRP type VM, but in this case, the sales order and dependent requirement quantities are included in the calculation. In this case, you are considering sales orders and dependent requirements that have consumed a portion of the forecast. This feature prevents over ordering.

- ▶ VV—Forecast-based planning—This selection will work similarly to the MRP type PD, where requirements are generated from a BOM explosion and net requirements calculation. However, the system is using the forecast from historical requirements data rather than actual customer orders to complete the planning run. In forecast planning, you must define the period pattern for the forecast. This can be monthly, weekly, daily, or per the defined accounting period. You must also define the number of periods you want included in the forecast. Each parameter is defined in the FORECASTING screen.

REORDER POINT—If you are using manual reorder point planning, you will enter the desired reorder point in this plant-specific field. If you are using automatic reorder point planning and maintaining a forecast, this field will be populated by the system and updated at a specified interval.

PLANNING TIME FENCE—If you are practicing master plan scheduling, you must define the period of time in workdays (standard days available for work per your plant calendar) in which no automatic changes will be made to the master schedule. The number of days you choose is entered in this plant-specific field. This will place into effect what planners refer to as the frozen zone.

PLANNING CYCLE—If you are practicing time-phased planning, you will be required to specify the day of the week or month in which the material is planned. That is done by assigning a planning cycle in this field, which must be maintained in SAP customizing. Time-phased planning is useful when continuously supplying the same customer. For instance, if you must deliver products to someone every Friday, you may be interested in time-phased planning.

> ## Reorder point planning has certain additional benefits
>
>  By setting very low-cost, high-use materials to reorder point planning, you can reduce material handling and empower shop floor employees. In this case, you allow production employees to make a reservation from inventory for a large amount of items that are commonly used in general production and set to reorder point planning, for example, inexpensive screws that may be used in producing several different products. This keeps the stock room from having to constantly issue screws with each work order and allows the production employee to keep moving in the event that a screw becomes damaged during the production process. A systematic requirement for this process is to also select the BULK MATERIAL indicator, which is defined in the MRP 2 screen (see Section 7.3.1).
>
> Another great use of reorder point planning is to reduce long lead times. If you are willing to take certain financial risk, you can set your items with the longest lead times to reorder point planning. This will ensure that those items are always in stock. Therefore, the critical path is now defined by materials within the BOM structure with shorter lead times. In this case, selecting the bulk material indicator is not required. Materials will not be withdrawn by reservation but rather through goods issue on the production order.

MRP CONTROLLER—This is where the MRP controller or group of controllers is assigned responsibility to the material. For an MRP controller to be assigned, it must first be maintained in SAP customizing. Just as we discussed with the purchasing group, it makes more sense to assign just one individual to a material so that responsibility is clearly defined and planners can be easily identified by others.

7.2.3 Lot size data

LOT SIZE—The selection you make in this plant-specific field will determine the lot size when a requirement is generated from the planning run. There are three lot sizing procedure types: static, periodic, and optimal.

There are several variations of each type to choose from to suit your needs.

- ▶ Static lot sizing procedures—The choices that pertain to this procedure are all relevant to quantity specifications in the material master. You can choose a fixed lot size, which is defined by quantity in the fixed lot size field. You can also choose lot-for-lot size, which makes the lot size of the material equal to its requirement minus the stock level (no rounding). Finally, you can select replenishment to the maximum stock level, which is used with reorder point planning MRP types to make up the difference between the current stock quantity and the maximum stock quantity that is defined in the maximum stock level field.

- ▶ Periodic lot sizing procedures—you can choose to group requirements together per day, week, month, or accounting period. In my organization, we use customized periodic lot sizing, where items are grouped together in period sizes that are dictated by the cost of the item. The more expensive the item is, the smaller the interval of time for grouping. For example, we may group together requirements for any item that costs less than $5 that lie in a sixty (60) day period. Conversely, we may group together requirements for any item that costs more than $1,000 in a ten (10) day period. This helps us to keep excess inventory costs to a minimum.

- ▶ Optimum lot sizing procedures—This method involves grouping lot sizes together based on economic ordering. For instance, one method is called the least unit cost procedure. This method takes storage time and storage costs into consideration when performing the lot size calculation.

MINIMUM LOT SIZE—The minimum quantity allowed for a lot size of any order. This quantity is taken into consideration when lot sizes are created for planned orders.

MAXIMUM LOT SIZE—The maximum quantity allowed for a lot size of any order. This quantity is taken into consideration when lot sizes are created for planned orders.

MAXIMUM STOCK LEVEL—If you are using the lot size procedure that replenishes stock to the maximum stock level, that maximum stock quantity must be maintained in this field.

ASSEMBLY SCRAP %—If you make a product that routinely experiences a scrap rate with every production lot, you can list the percent that is scrapped in every production lot. The system will over-plan the lot size accordingly. For instance, if you list the scrap percentage as 5% a requirement for 40 items will be planned as a lot size of 42.

TAKT TIME—If your lot size is limited by your lot size procedure (most likely due to capacity constraints), yet you require more items than the maximum quantity allowed per the procedure, you can apply an overlapping rule to the lot size procedure in SAP customizing. This will allow several lots to be planned within the same period that are under the maximum lot size. Those lots will be separated in planning date by the number of working days that you enter in this field. It should be the amount of time it takes to produce one lot.

For those of you working in a lean environment, where takt time is calculated in minutes or seconds, this is not the field you are looking for. SAP offers several lean solutions to manage your shop floor control. I recommend investigating the Kanban feature that SAP offers to manage your pull system.

ROUNDING PROFILE—This field was previously defined in Chapter 5. It has been included here because the field can apply to rounding in delivery quantity proposals, as well as planned order quantities. For more information, see the explanation for a static rounding profile in Section 5.2.3.

ROUNDING VALUE—If you are not maintaining a rounding profile, you can use this plant-specific field to round up your planned order and requisition quantities. If your requirement is less than the specified value, your planned requirement is rounded up to that value. If your requirements quantity exceeds the rounding value, the requirement will be rounded up to the next multiple of the rounding value. This field can be useful in resource management.

Case example: Lot sizing

 Alex is the materials planner for a large sewing work center that produces a well-established line of men's jackets. With an abundance of sewers available, resource capacity is not an issue for Alex, so he practices infinite capacity planning. This means that he can add or remove sewers to the work center according to the daily production requirements. Based on time studies over the years, it has been consistently proven that one sewer can produce 20 jackets per day. Therefore, Alex wants his production requirements to be grouped per day in multiples relevant to the resource capabilities. To accomplish this, Alex sets his lot size to a daily (TB) grouping. He also sets his rounding value to 20. These settings will result in one planned order each day that is issued in multiples of 20. Now the sewing supervisor can easily assign the appropriate number of resources to production at the beginning of each day with confidence that the work will be completed by the end of the shift. If Alex should ever find that his resource capacity has been limited to a certain number, he can apply a cap to the quantity of the daily planned orders by setting that value in the maximum lot size field.

UNIT OF MEASURE GROUP—This is the same field that was defined in Chapter 5. For more information, see Section 5.2.1. It is applicable to rounding profile.

> ## Use your lot size settings to determine your costing lot size
>
>  In order to perform cost estimates in SAP, you must maintain a costing lot size (see Chapter 10). It only makes sense to choose a costing lot size that closely or exactly matches the lot size that you normally produce or procure. Furthermore, you will have to use a costing lot size that fits within the structure of your purchasing information record if you are maintaining scaled pricing. Let the settings that you have made in lot size determination help guide your costing lot size choice. This will enable you to produce more accurate and error free cost estimates.

7.2.4 MRP areas

MRP AREA EXISTS indicator—By selecting this indicator, you are stating that special MRP parameters will be applied to this material during the planning run. Those parameters can be entered by selecting the MRP AREAS icon to the right (see Figure 7.1). You must maintain the necessary MRP profiles in SAP customizing in order for them to appear as a selection here.

7.3 MRP 2 screen

There are three information sets within the MRP 2 screen (see Figure 7.2): PROCUREMENT, SCHEDULING, and NET REQUIREMENTS CALCULATION. The procurement section is where you select your make/buy decision, as well as make some storage location choices. The scheduling information set is where you set your lead time data. Finally, the net requirements calculation information set enables you to define requirements calculations to ensure your desired level of customer satisfaction.

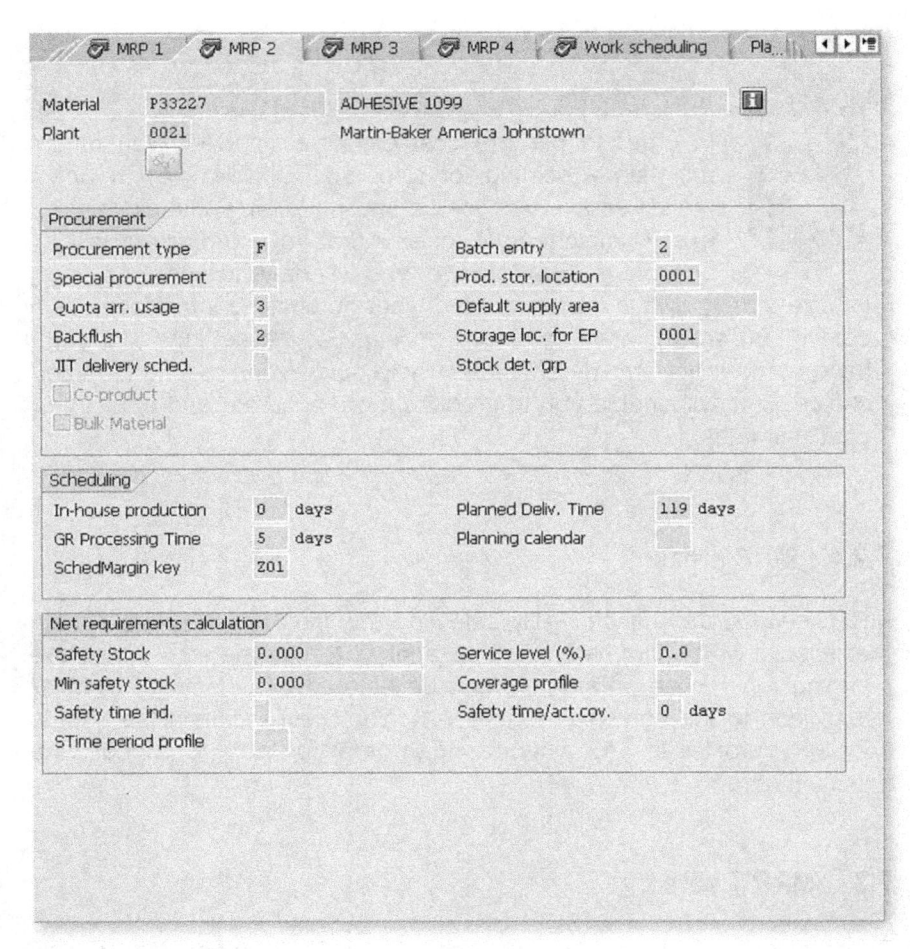

Figure 7.2: MRP 2 screen

7.3.1 Procurement

PROCUREMENT TYPE—This plant-specific field is where the make/buy decision is made. You will have three choices available in material types pertaining to production: external procurement, internally produced, or both.

▶ Procured externally—If you are procuring an item externally, the system searches your purchasing info records to make a vendor selection for planning data. If you have more than one approved vendor for a given material, you must choose wh ch vendor will be used as the default vendor for planning in ycur source list. Depending on your level of automation, MRP may generate planned orders, purchase requisitions, or purchase orders for externally procured materials during the planning run. The lead time used in the MRP calculation is stored in the PLANNED DELIVERY TIME field within the scheduling information set.

▶ Internally produced—If you select this choice, the system will search for an available BOM and routing to schedule planned production orders. The BOM and routing to be used for MRP calculations must be defined in the production version within the MRP 4 screen. You may maintain several production versions within the same validity period. If more than one s valid at the time of the planning run, the system simply selects the first production version listed for MRP calculations. The lead time used in the MRP calculation can either be stored in the in-house production time field within the scheduling information set, or you can allow the system to calculate the lead time from router data. If you make the latter choice, you must update the in-house production time in days information set within the WORK SCHEDULING screen. See Section 7.7.3 for more information on lead time scheduling.

▶ Both external procurement and internally produced—This selection can be used if you both make and buy a material. Here, the system uses the PLANNED DELIVERY TIME field to make its MRP calculation. The planning run will generate planned orders to fulfill requirements and you must choose whether to create a production order or a purchasing requisition. If you are maintaining a quota arrangement, you can specify the distribution of make versus buy as a percentage.

BATCH ENTRY—This plant-specific field is used to specify how batches of components that you issue to a work order are determined. If you are requiring batch entries, you can choose to have them automatically assigned, manually assigned before the release of the order, or manually assigned before the goods issue of the order. You may alsc make a selection that states that batches can be entered before goods issue, but not required. The choice you make ultimately depends on your inventory traceability policy and the point in the parts picking process where you want your systematic batch checking to occur.

SPECIAL PROCUREMENT—This plant-specific field allows you to more precisely define your procurement type. You will have many standard choices available, ranging from a consignment material to a phantom assembly. There are also choices in this field that will allow procurement from another plant's production line. See the Bonus section—Subcontracting procurement for a detailed look at a great Special Procurement field opportunity.

Case example: Special procurement

Stanley is the continuous improvement officer for a production facility that makes remote control airplanes. He has been tasked with removing wasteful activities from the production process. By evaluating the value stream, he has found that the airplanes are manufactured in several stages, where several subassemblies are built on their own production orders and sent to inventory prior to being issued to the final assembly production order. The process was established this way to allow the sale of those subassemblies from inventory for customer repairs, but those occurrences are rare. Stanley realizes that he can reduce material handling and lead time by producing the entire assembly on one production order. This will allow the stock room to pick and stock materials only once per production lot. However, he must somehow maintain the ability to sell those subassemblies as a spare component when necessary. Stanley decides to assign the special procurement code phantom assembly (50) to each subassembly material master. This effectively removes the subassembly from having planned order generated and places the components of each subassembly into the top-level BOM. Now all components required to make the full assembly are issued to the top-level production order. If a requirement is entered for any given subassembly, Stanley still has the ability to issue a production order and inventory the subassembly, but has reduced the wasteful activities from the normal production process.

Bonus section—Subcontracting procurement

The current manufacturing environment requires us to function in a global supply chain, where geographic and cultural limitations must be overcome and only organizations that are flexible and adaptable will survive. As material buyers, we must employ technological tools that facilitate this necessary flexibility. One of those tools offered by SAP is the subcontracting purchase order. This process works much like a standard purchase order. However, a subcontracting purchase order allows you to provide raw and component materials from your own inventory to an outside vendor for further processing. Once the vendor is finished, you will then receive the completed material into inventory from the subcontracting purchase order.

When to use subcontracting purchase orders

The subcontracting purchase order is useful for many reasons. Here are some likely scenarios:

▶ You are working with a small vendor that might have the necessary core competencies that you require, but not the operating cash to afford the upfront raw material costs.

▶ You want to expedite work at a vendor's location by supplying them with material that you have on hand.

▶ You are the channel master in an extended supply chain and control the flow of all materials and processes in the chain.

Now that we've covered the potential uses of a subcontracting purchase order, let's address how to create one. In order to create subcontracting purchase orders, you will need to make some adjustments in the material master, create a bill of material, create a purchasing information record capable of subcontracting, and issue the necessary materials to the subcontracting vendor.

Subcontracting PO—material master setup

The adjustments required in the material master are quite simple. There are two screens within the material master that will require adjustment. First, access the material master of the material you wish to have sub-contracted through SAP transaction MM02 and go to the MRP 2 screen. Select code (30) for subcontracting in the SPECIAL PROCUREMENT field (see Figure 7.3). By making this selection, you are telling MRP that a bill of material is to be considered when performing requirements planning.

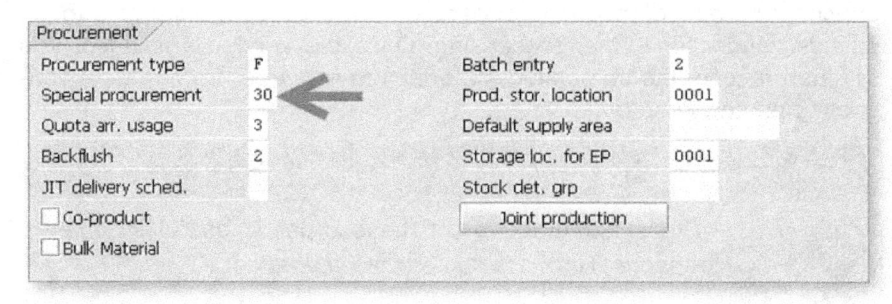

Figure 7.3: MRP 2 screen—special procurement

Secondly, access the COSTING 1 screen of the material master. Here you will also add the subcontracting code (30) to the SPECIAL PROCUREMENT COSTING field (see Figure 7.4). This selection will allow for the appropriate subcontracting costing structure to be generated when performing your cost estimating in SAP transaction CK11N. This costing structure will look a bit different than the usual purchased components in CK11N, because it will now list the sub-components from the bill of material that you will create for this effort in a parent/child relationship.

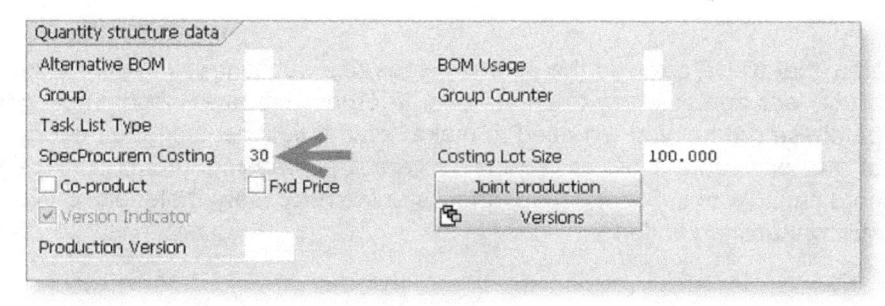

Figure 7.4: Costing 1 screen—special procurement costing

Subcontracting PO—create a bill of material (BOM)

In order to provide materials to a vendor and link those materials to the subcontracting purchase order, you will need to create a BOM. This BOM will be no different than any other BOM you might create. Simply go to SAP transaction CS01 and create a BOM for the parent material that you wish to have completed by your subcontracting vendor. In the example (see Figure 7.5), you will see that we wish to have our vendor complete the material B1234 with material sub-components C4567 and D8901 that are being supplied by our organization.

Warning: Bulk material indicator

tems marked as "bulk material" are not possible for use in a subcontracting BOM. Look at the "bulk material" indicator in the MRP 2 screen of the material master to be sure.

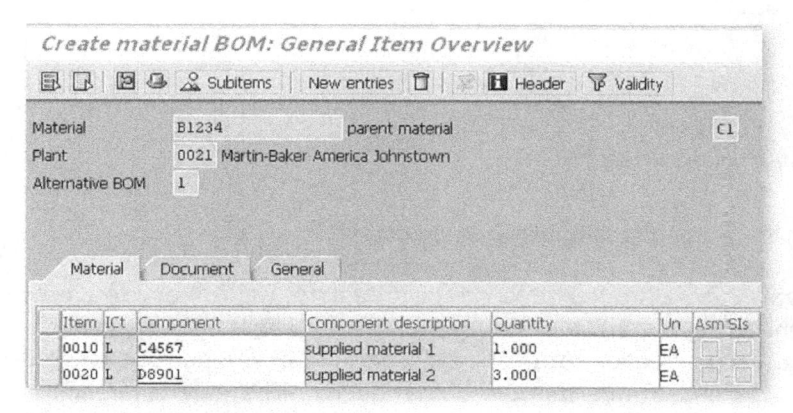

Figure 7.5: Subcontracting BOM

Subcontracting PO—create a purchasing information record (PIR)

The final setup step in the process is to create a subcontracting PIR for the vendor that will be performing the process. The steps to create this PIR are the same as any PIR you might create, but with one very important difference. When creating your subcontracting PIR, you must select the SUBCONTRACTING feature in the opening screen of SAP transaction ME11 (see Figure 7.6). By creating a subcontracting PIR, you are telling the MRP system to create requisitions that are linked to sub-components when this particular vendor is selected as the source of supply. Therefore, when requisitions are converted to purchase orders, and the sub-component materials are issued to those purchase orders, those sub-component materials will be allocated to that particular vendor in SAP inventory management.

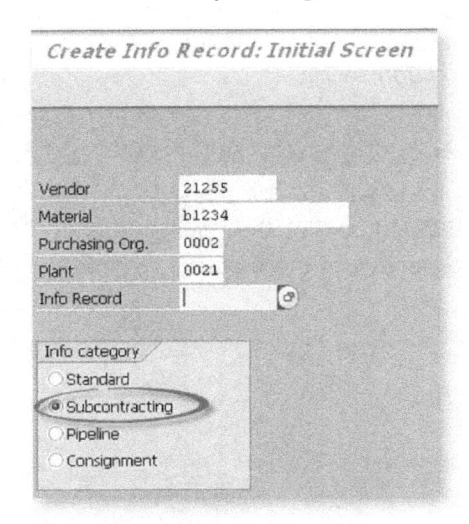

Figure 7.6: Subcontracting PIR

Creating the subcontracting PO / issuing material

Now that we've set up the subcontracting feature, we're ready to create a subcontracting purchase order. It's really quite similar to any standard purchase order creation. You will still convert MRP-generated requisitions into purchase orders in the same fashion. The only difference is that now you will have to issue the raw material to the purchase order upon creation. The following step-by-step procedure will show you how.

Begin by going to SAP transaction MB1B (see Figure 7.7). Enter today's date in the DOCUMENT DATE field and your desired posting date in the POSTING DATE field. Next enter movement type 541 in the MOVEMENT TYPE field, as well as your desired plant and storage location in their respective fields, and click on the TO PURCHASE ORDER icon.

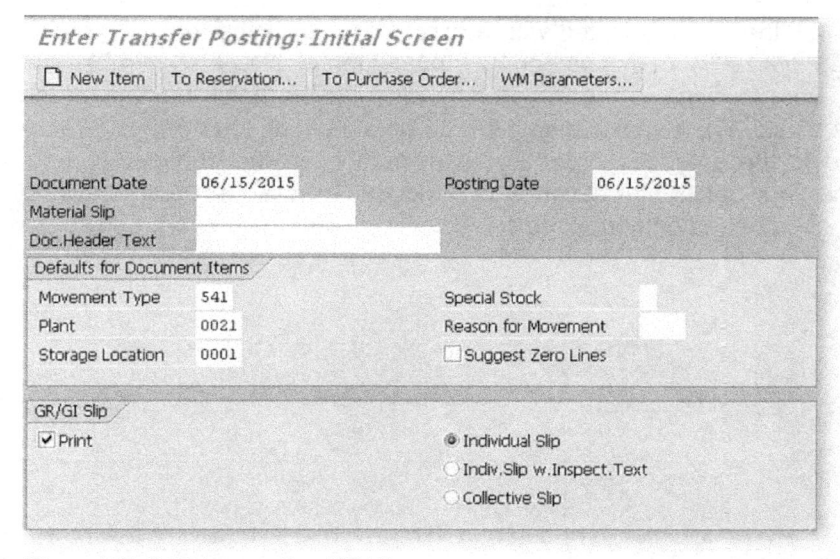

Figure 7.7: SAP transaction MB1B

A popup box will appear (see Figure 7.8). Here you will enter your PO and item number and click the ADOPT + DETAILS icon.

Figure 7.8: MB1B popup screen

You will then be presented with a screen to initiate the transfer posting (see Figure 7.9). In this screen, you must identify the batch number that you want to issue to the supplier by entering the batch number in the BATCH field. The remaining data will be defaulted for you from your reference to the purchase order and item number in the previous screen. Once your batch information is entered, click the ADOPT icon shown in the top left-hand portion of the screen.

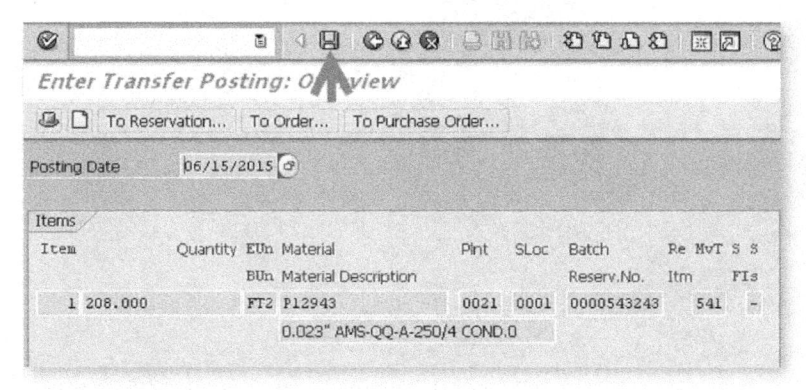

Figure 7.9: MB1B—transfer posting

You will finally be taken to the next screen (see Figure 7.10), where you must click on the POST icon to complete the issuance of goods.

Figure 7.10: MB1B—post goods issue

Your material has now been issued to the purchase order. But, note that your transfer posting rules may require you to perform further processing in SAP transaction LT01 to clear this movement from an inventory transfer area.

Example

Marcus has been appointed to the position of supply chain manager at an auto parts manufacturing company. He has been told that he will be responsible for reducing plant-wide material costs by 10% as his first task. Marcus begins his analysis to look for redundancies in the supply chain and other non-value added activities. It is not long before he realizes that there is inefficiency in system-wide raw material purchases. He finds that nearly every one of his suppliers purchases the same grade of aluminum to make their components. However, the quantity of material that each supplier procures is not enough to qualify for a volume discount and that high cost is passed along to the auto parts manufacturer. Marcus knows that supply chain costs can be leveraged by developing strategic partnerships and integrating those partners. He decides to integrate the procurement process for all suppliers who are using the same raw aluminum. He does this, in part, by using the SAP subcontracting purchase order feature. First, he asks his subcontractors to quote a price for the necessary components, and not include the cost of raw material in their quote. Secondly, he configures each of those components to be scheduled in his MRP using the special procurement feature (subcontracting) with the necessary raw material BOM in place for the raw aluminum. Now Marcus is capable of collecting all periodic requirements for the common aluminum that is required for his supply chain. He now has the volume required for discounted raw material prices. He enhances this process by directing the raw material to be drop-shipped to each subcontractor per line item of the raw material purchase. This gives him control and visibility on the delivery timing of the raw material. Finally, he places subcontracting purchase orders with those component suppliers, in which case Marcus's firm has provided the raw material at a discounted rate, thereby reducing cost of goods sold across the supply chain.

PRODUCTION STORAGE LOCATION—This plant-specific field defines the storage location where a material is stored if it is produced in-house. If the material is a component of a BOM, this is the location that the component is issued from. If the material is an assembly being produced, this is the location where it will be stored.

QUOTA ARRANGEMENT USAGE—This is the same field that was defined in Chapter 6. For more information, see Section 6.2.3. This field has been included here for reference to its application in quota arrangements that use both in-house production and external procurement.

DEFAULT SUPPLY AREA—This plant-specific field is used to define storage locations that exist on the production floor. If you are in a lean environment, this is yet another effective SAP function to facilitate your lean process. It is used for Kanban replenishment calculations, as well as an area from which to pull materials from during the Kanban production process.

BACKFLUSH—Backflushing is the process of relieving inventory when a component is consumed on a production order. You can specify when the backflush will take place during the processing or a production or process order in the routing for the assembly being produced. In this field, you can choose to always backflush the material, or you can choose to determine backflushing rules in each work center.

STORAGE LOCATION FOR EXTERNAL PROCUREMENT—This plant-specific field can be used to specifically define a storage location for externally procured items during planned order generation. This is useful in guiding material deliveries to their intended destination within large production facilities.

JUST-IN-TIME DELIVERY SCHEDULE indicator—This is the same field that was defined in Chapter 6. For more information, see Section 6.2.3. This field has been included here for its reference to your lean production environment.

STOCK DETERMINATION GROUP—This plant-specific field is used to select a stock determination group, which is defined in customization, to work in conjunction with a stock determination rule. Together, these settings will determine stocking procedures for a given material. This feature is used in repetitive manufacturing, where stock determinations must be defined.

CO-PRODUCT indicator—A co-product is a material that is produced as the result of producing another item. For instance, the production of certain chemicals may also result in the yield of other useful chemicals. You can create co-products by selecting this indicator in both materials to be produced by the same production or process order. This process has far reaching implications into costing and settlement. Therefore, some work is required in SAP customizing in regard to order settlement and goods receipts for this process to work.

BULK MATERIAL indicator—Set this plant-specific indicator to active for materials that you want to be continuously available at the work center. For instance, you may use a certain adhesive in most of the products produced in a given work center. You will want your operators to have constant access to the adhesive. Therefore, your operators will make reservations for this material when they need more, rather than having small quantities issued with each production order.

If a material should always be treated as a bulk material, you should activate the indicator in the material master. If an item is only used as a bulk material occasionally, you can set the bulk material indicator as active in the relevant BOM. A condition of a bulk material is that it is planned using a reorder point (consumption based planning) and a net requirement calculation will not be performed for the material during the planning run. This means that the material will be expensed to your desired cost center ledger account at the time of reservation and not applied as a direct cost to the production order you are using it on.

7.3.2 Scheduling

IN-HOUSE PRODUCTION—You can define the lead time of your in-house production for a given material in two ways. One choice is to maintain a time in work days in this field, which is independent of lot size. Alternatively, you can maintain the setup, interoperation processing time, and processing time in the in-house production time in the day's information set of the WORK SCHEDULING screen. If you choose the latter option, those values can be updated in the material master for you from information in the router. In this case, scheduling is determined using the specified lot sizing.

Use the WORK SCHEDULING screen to manage production lead time

 For those of us concerned with defining and evaluating value-added activities, maintaining the in-house production field for production lead time is not detailed enough. Maintaining the lot size dependent production lead time through the WORK SCHEDULING screen allows for more detail and accuracy in planning. By maintaining the lot independent in-house production time, you are only saying that the entire process takes a certain number of working days. The lead time calculation process consists of several fixed and variable elements, which you are not describing in detail when using this field. Conversely, by using the values from the production router, you can discern setup from processing time in your continuous improvement evaluations. You can also better plan your capacity by using lot-size-dependent data. Furthermore, you will have the ability to update lead time data for all materials with a mass change through another SAP transaction by having the system review the current production routers. For more information on lot size dependent lead time, see Section 7.7.3.

PLANNED DELIVERY TIME—This plant-specific field is the number of calendar days it takes to receive an externally procured material from the time it is ordered. The value you enter here is used for requirements scheduling in your MRP run. If you have several vendors that supply a given material, SAP recommends that you use an average of all vendors' quoted lead times. However, I suggest that you use the longest quoted lead time of the group. This will ensure on-time delivery in all cases.

GOODS RECEIPT PROCESSING TIME—In this plant-specific field, you can define the number of work days that it takes to receive and inspect an item before it is placed into stock. In this case, using an average time based on historical data may be prudent. This value is also included in the scheduling data during your MRP run.

PLANNING CALENDAR—If you are using periodic lot sizing per a planning calendar or time-phased planning, you must specify the planning calendar to be used for the material in this field.

SCHEDULE MARGIN KEY—The key you enter in this plant-specific field will consist of a group of float time values. That is, time in work days that you want to add as a buffer in lead time scheduling to allow for administrative activities. For example, you can place a float time in the release period to allow a set number of days for your buyer to react to a requisition or for your materials planner to convert a planned order to a production order. This time is then factored into the overall lead time scheduling so that you do not compromise the order's due date while waiting for administrative tasks to be performed. Each key is defined in SAP customizing and consists of values for four different types of float periods: opening period, float after production, float before production, and release period.

7.3.3 Net requirements calculation

SAFETY STOCK—Used mostly in make-to-stock environments, this is the amount of stock that you want to carry at all times to satisfy irregularly high demand. It is most useful in automatic reorder point planning in a forecast system. In this case, the safety stock value is recalculated for you by using the defined service level. It can also be used in manual reorder point planning, but be careful, the safety stock value in this case is for information only and will not be used in net requirements calculations.

SERVICE LEVEL (%)—This is the level of customer orders that you want to be able to satisfy from inventory. The percentage that you enter in this plant-specific field will be used to calculate your safety stock if you are using the forecast system. The higher the service level, the more safety stock you will maintain.

MINIMUM SAFETY STOCK—This is simply the low limit that you place on safety stock for forecasting. If the safety stock is calculated to be below this value, the system will reevaluate and set the safety stock to the defined minimum value.

COVERAGE PROFILE—This profile can be created in SAP customizing to create a dynamic safety stock on the basis of average daily demand within a defined period. Those tracking seasonal demand trends may find this field beneficial.

SAFETY TIME indicator—If you are using safety time, the selection you make in this plant-specific field will determine what type of requirements are brought forward in time by your defined safety time. You can choose to include safety time for independent requirements or safety time for all requirements.

SAFETY TIME / ACTUAL RANGE OF COVERAGE—This is where you define the number of days you want to bring your planning data forward to account for safety time. The actual requirement dates of your orders are not changed, but are scheduled inwards according to the number of days you enter here.

SAFETY TIME PERIOD PROFILE—This field is used to assign a profile that differs from your standard safety time range of coverage. It is used to handle exceptional or seasonal demand in a known and defined period. For example, you can make the range of coverage larger in October for costume accessories and maintain a standard profile for the rest of the year.

7.4 MRP 3 screen

The MRP 3 screen (see Figure 7.11) contains four information sets: FORECAST REQUIREMENTS, PLANNING, AVAILABILITY CHECK, and PLANT SPE-CIFIC CONFIGURATION. The fields within the forecast requirements information set are required when maintaining a forecast and will help to define the forecast intervals. The planning information set is where you choose your planning strategy and requirements consumption characteristics. In the availability check information set, you will define how the system ensures that requirements can be met. Finally, the plant-specific configuration information set is used to plan material variants at the plant level in an assemble-to-order environment.

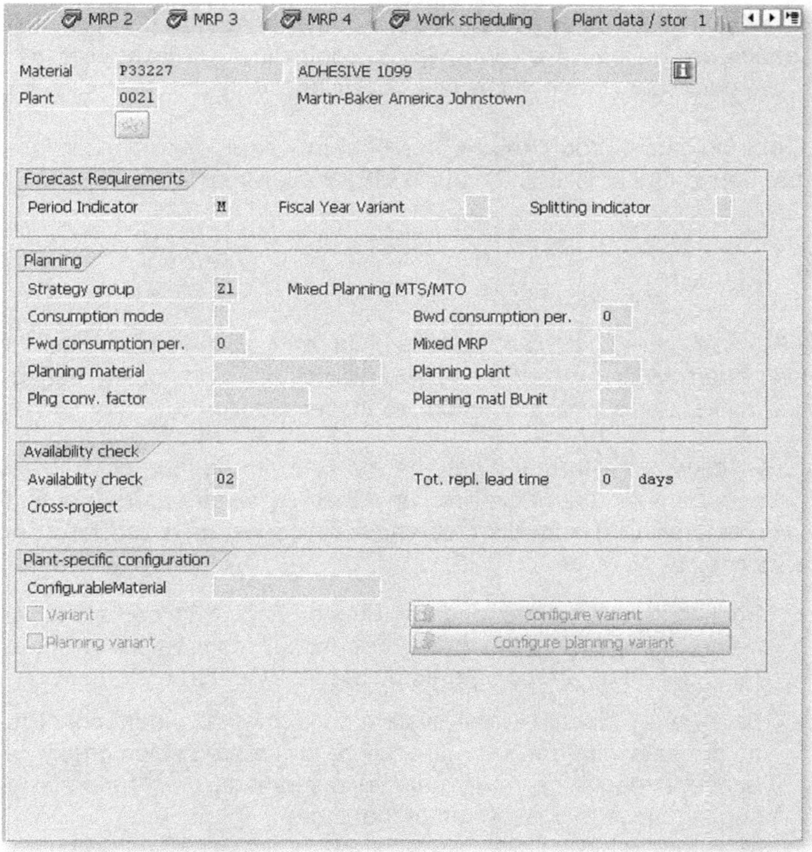

Figure 7.11: MRP 3 screen

7.4.1 Forecast requirements

PERIOD indicator—If you are using forecasting, you must choose the interval in which the forecast and consumption values are calculated. You can choose daily, weekly, or monthly periods. Alternatively, you can use more customized periods by selecting fiscal year variant or planning calendar periods.

FISCAL YEAR VARIANT—This field can be used to define how many posting periods and special periods are allocated to the fiscal year if you want them to differ from the standard fiscal year. You can have up to 16 periods in a fiscal year. Setting up fiscal year variants require that the posting periods are defined the same way in controlling, as fiscal year variants have consequences in financial accounting.

SPLITTING indicator—You can use this field to further dissect your forecast per period into smaller intervals in MRP requirements planning.

7.4.2 Planning

STRATEGY GROUP—This plant-specific field is where you choose the planning strategy for a given material. This field was previously defined in detail in Chapter 3. For more information, see Section 3.2.

CONSUMPTION MODE—In this plant-specific field, you can choose if and how independent requirements are consumed by sales orders, dependent requirements, and material reservations. You will have the following standard choices.

- ▶ Backward only—Independent requirements with dates that lie before an entered sales order, dependent requirement, or material reservation are consumed by the newly entered element.

- ▶ Backward / forward—The system consumes all independent requirements with dates that lie before an entered sales order, dependent requirement, or material reservation date before consuming those that lie ahead of that date.

- ▶ Forward only—Independent requirements with dates that lie after an entered sales order, dependent requirement, or material reservation are consumed by the newly entered requirement.

- ▶ Forward / backward—The system consumes all independent requirements with dates that lie after an entered sales order, dependent requirement, or material reservation date before consuming those that lie before that date.

BACKWARDS CONSUMPTION PERIOD—If you are using backwards consumption, you must specify how far back in time independent requirements are to be consumed. This period is defined in calendar days. You can go as far back as 999 days.

FORWARDS CONSUMPTION PERIOD—If you are using forwards consumption, you must specify how far ahead in time independent requirements are to be consumed. This period is defined in calendar days. You can go as far forward as 999 days

MIXED MRP indicator—This field can be used in a make-to-stock environment where you want to control how subassemblies are planned with the final assembly or gross requirement. For example, if you are forecasting the final assembly, you may want your subassembly quantities recalculated when independent requirements are consumed at the final assembly level when a customer order is received.

PLANNING MATERIAL—A planning material is a material master created to plan the basic requirements of a configurable material. The idea is that the planning material is used to plan the non-variant, or standard, components of the configurable material. The planning material is never actually produced, it is only planned.

If you are using a planning strategy that involves a planning material, you will need to enter the planning material in this field for the non-variant component of the configurable material to be sold. This way, when a customer order is received for a given, configurable material, the independent requirements of the defined planning material are consumed. For more information on planning material consumption see Section 3.2.2.

PLANNING PLANT—This is the plant where the independent requirements of your planning material will come from.

PLANNING CONVERSION FACTOR—In SAP customizing, you can define a conversion factor to convert the base unit of measure of the given material into the base unit of measure of the planning material. You can enter that conversion factor here. Otherwise, the system searches its own conversion tables.

PLANNING MATERIAL BASE UNIT OF MEASURE—This is the base unit of measure as defined in the planning material's material master. It is copied here for reference once a planning material has been assigned.

7.4.3 Availability check

AVAILABILITY CHECK—This is the same field that was defined in Chapter 5. For more information, see Section 5.4.1. This field was included here for its reference to materials planning.

TOTAL REPLENISHMENT LEAD TIME—This plant-specific field is used to depict the overall lead time of a material produced in-house by adding all of lead times from the material's exploded BOM that are on the critical path. This total replenishment lead time should include planned delivery times and in-house production times, as well as goods receipt processing times. When the system completes an availability check, it looks to this field first. If this field is not maintained, the system only uses the in-house production time required to produce the given item and does not consider the replenishment time for components during the availability check. This field is not calculated by SAP, rather it is a manual entry made by the end user in work days. When performing an availability check on a procured item, the system simply looks to the schedule margin key, planned delivery time, and goods receipt processing time in the material master.

Total replenishment lead time helps to ensure on time delivery

 You can eliminate a good amount of leg work in sales and operations planning by maintaining a total replenishment lead time for all sellable materials. If you've maintained the field, any SAP user can see when the material will be available again by clicking on the SHOW TOTAL REPLENISHMENT LEAD TIME icon (see Figure 7.12) in the STOCK DETAILS screen (SAP transaction MD04). Once you click this icon, the date on which the material can be available again is shown in blue (see Figure 7.13). Furthermore, the system will not allow anyone to enter the material for sale within the total replenishment lead time.

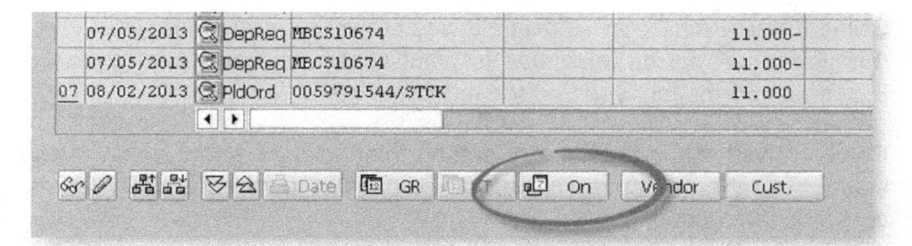

	07/05/2013	DepReq	MBCS10674		11.000-
	07/05/2013	DepReq	MBCS10674		11.000-
07	08/02/2013	PldOrd	0059791544/STCK		11.000

Figure 7.12: Total replenishment lead time icon

Stock/Requirements List as of 10:32 hrs

Show Overview Tree   Customer Pegging   Month Due

Material	MBCS12060	PLATFORM ASSY SITTING		
MRP area	0021	Martin-Baker America Johnstown		
Plant	0021	MRP type PD Material Type HALB Unit

E	Date	A	MRP el	MRP element data	Reschedulin	Receipt/Reqmt
	01/03/2014		DepReq	MBCS10674		11.000-
	01/03/2014		DepReq	MBCS10674		11.000-
	01/03/2014		DepReq	MBCS10674		11.000-
	01/03/2014		DepReq	MBCS10674		11.000-
	01/21/2014		---->	End of Replen. Lead		
	02/03/2014		PldOrd	0059791597/STCK		11.000

Figure 7.13: Availability date

CROSS-PROJECT indicator—You can use this plant-specific indicator to determine whether inventory outside of the project account assignment should be considered in the availability check.

7.4.4 Plant-specific configuration

CONFIGURABLE MATERIAL—As I described in Chapter 4, there are two types of configurable materials: cross-plant materials and plant-specific materials. This information set controls plant-specific configurable materials, which is valid for use in your particular plant only. For more information on configurable materials, see Section 4.3.5.

MATERIAL IS A VARIANT indicator—This field was previously defined in Chapter 4. It is listed here for its relevance to plant-specific material configuration. For more information, see Section 4.3.5.

CONFIGURE VARIANT icon—This field was previously defined in Chapter 4. It is listed here for its relevance to plant-specific material configuration. For more information, see Section 4.3.5.

PLANNING VARIANT indicator—By setting this indicator as active, you are stating that the configurable material is used to plan other BOM items critical to production.

CONFIGURE PLANNING VARIANT icon—By clicking this icon you will be taken to a screen where you can define the planning variant of the configurable material.

7.5 MRP 4 screen

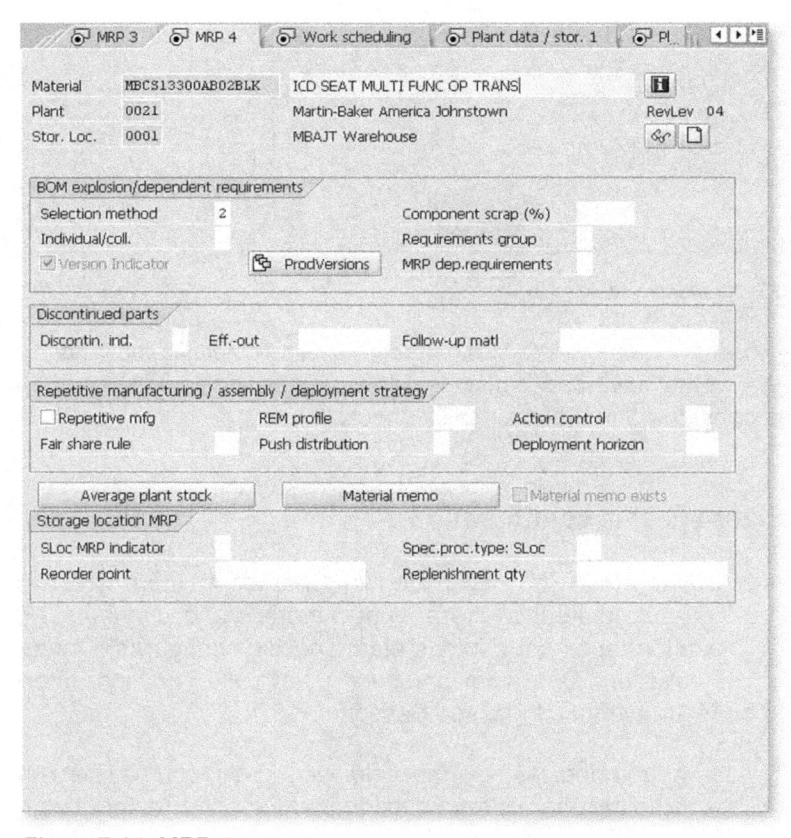

Figure 7.14: MRP 4 screen

The MRP 4 screen (see Figure 7.14) contains four information sets: BOM EXPLOSION / DEPENDENT REQUIREMENTS, DISCONTINUED PARTS, REPETITIVE MANUFACTURING / ASSEMBLY / DEPLOYMENT STRATEGY, and STORAGE LOCATION MRP. The fields within the BOM explosion information set helps you to select the appropriate BOM and routing necessary to produce a component, as well as group requirements for production planning. The discontinued parts information set helps you to transition replacement items into production for parts that will no longer be used. Obviously, the repetitive manufacturing information set is for use in repetitive production environments. And finally, the storage location MRP information set is used when you are defining special storage locations for materials within your plant.

7.5.1 BOM explosion/dependent requirements

SELECTION METHOD—It is not uncommon to maintain several different bills of material for an item produced in-house. You will choose the method of BOM selection in this plant-specific field. There are four possible selections.

- ▶ Selection by order quantity—If you are using this method, you will maintain several BOMs, each of which will have a valid lot size range. The BOM selected for use in production will depend on the lot size quantity of the planned order. This can be useful if you store inventory in location according to its volume. That way, if an order quantity exceeds a certain size, the inventory is pulled from a larger storage location.

- ▶ Selection by explosion date—By using this method, you will be using the BOM that is valid by date at the time of selection. This is useful when you want to cut in new components to replace old ones at a known date.

- ▶ Selection by production version—This selection is used when you are maintaining production versions. You can have more than one valid production version at a time. If you do have more than one valid production version at a time, the system chooses the first one in the list. You can alter which production version is used, thereby controlling which BOM is selected by choosing that particular production version in the planned order and firming the order. If no production version exists, the system searches for a valid BOM.

▶ Selection by production version only—This is the same as selection by production version, but if a valid production version does not exist, the system will not allow a production or process order to be created.

COMPONENT SCRAP (%)—By entering a percentage here, the quantity of this material issued to a BOM is increased by that percentage to account for a known scrap rate during production.

INDIVIDUAL / COLLECTIVE REQUIREMENTS—The choice you make in this plant-specific field determines how your dependent requirements are grouped together. That is, if two different customer orders are entered, you can decide if you want the planned orders and requisitions for the components to be grouped together or not. In a simple environment, where you want to make efficient production runs, it makes sense to collect the requirements together. In other situations, like sales order stock, where you are building inventory directly for a particular sales order, you must select individual requirements. You can also select both individual and collective requirements, which can be used for mixed MRP types where you sometimes want individual requirements and sometimes want collective requirements.

REQUIREMENTS GROUP—If you want to display all dependent requirements per day in a list on the STOCK DETAILS screen that tells you how many requirements you have per day, you can select that option in this plant-specific field (see Figure 7.15). This does not affect how requirements are scheduled and is only a view preference.

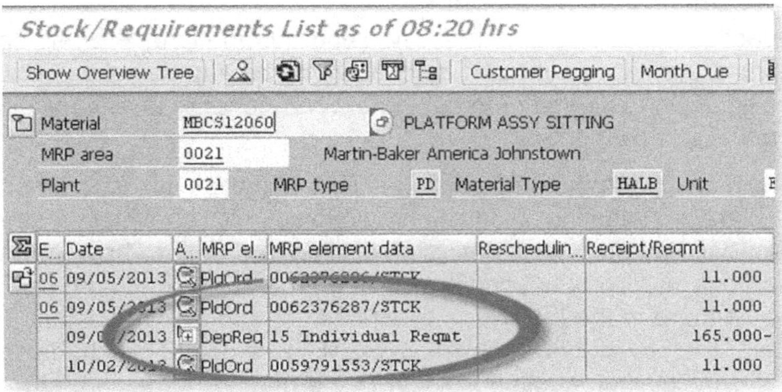

Figure 7.15: Requirements grouping

VERSION indicator—This indicator will be active if you have created a production version. It can be useful for reporting.

PRODUCTION VERSIONS icon—By clicking on this icon, you can create, change, and view your production versions. A production version is used to tie a BOM and router together for a production recipe. There are other assignment features available within each production version (see Figure 7.16). Each production version you create must have a valid date range, but as I mentioned before, you can have more than one valid version at a time. Production versions are a necessary element if you are performing costing by product cost collector.

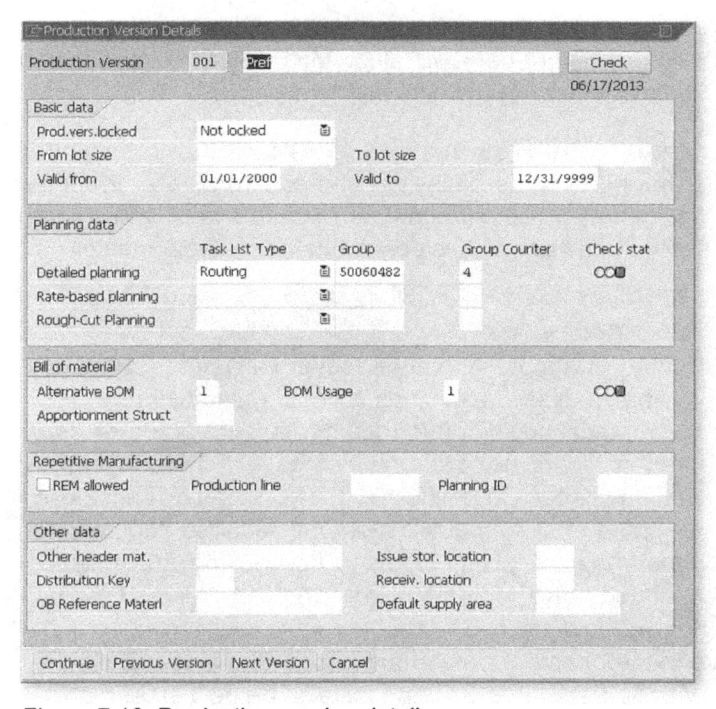

Figure 7.16: Production version details

MRP DEPENDENT REQUIREMENTS indicator—If you are planning at the assembly level in a make-to-stock environment, you may want to set this indicator so MRP-dependent requirements are not planned. This will prevent your independent requirements from being over planned if you have other dependent requirements, like a material reservation.

7.5.2 Discontinued parts

The next three fields work together to maintain a continuous supply of an item, when one material is acceptable to replace another. For example, you may want to replace an item that is obsolete with newer technology. By maintaining these three fields, the dependent requirements of the discontinued material will be transferred to the follow up material in MRP planning when the discontinued material stock is depleted.

DISCONTINUATION indicator—Set the indicator if you are discontinuing and replacing the given material

EFFECTIVE OUT DATE—If you want to plan a replacement in the distant future, using the effective out date will allow MRP to continue planning the discontinued material up until the specified date.

FOLLOW UP MATERIAL—This is the material to replace the discontinued material. It must have the same base unit of measure as the discontinued material. You can also assign follow up materials in a BOM, which has a higher priority than that which is defined in the material master.

Case example: Discontinued part

Brittney is a material planner/buyer for a production facility that makes brake lines for car manufacturers. Her raw material supplier informed her that the grade of steel used to fabricate the brake lines will no longer be available after December 31st. The supplier intends to carry a cheaper grade of steel that will meet the required engineering standards. Brittney has the ability to plan ahead using the material master's discontinued parts information set. She first creates the material master for the new steel. She then sets the DISCONTINUED indicator to active in the old steel's material master. She also installs the effective-out date as December 31st and installs the new steel material number in the FOLLOW-ON MATERIAL field. Brittney has now ensured continuous planning, and as a result, continuous supply of the required raw material. As an added bonus, Brittney can now use the old steel's material number as a forecast model for the new steel by placing the old material number in the reference material for consumption field of the FORECASTING screen (see Section 7.6.1).

7.5.3 Repetitive manufacturing / assembly / deployment strategy

REPETITIVE MANUFACTURING indicator—Setting this plant-specific indicator allows for backflushing in repetitive manufacturing. It also requires that you maintain a repetitive manufacturing profile.

REPETITIVE MANUFACTURING PROFILE—Your profiles are defined in SAP customizing to control how materials are backflushed, and other activities, such as which goods movement types are used in issues and receipts.

ACTION CONTROL—Repetitive manufacturing can require processes that span a large geographic area. For that reason, you may want to trigger certain SAP activities by specified production activities. Events like backflushing can be triggered through an online interface.

FAIR SHARE RULE—This rule is used to distribute inventory if there is not enough stock to satisfy all demand. You can choose to either distribute the available inventory proportionately amongst the distribution channels according to demand, or distribute the available stock as an equal percentage of the channels target stock value.

PUSH DISTRIBUTION indicator—You can use this field to handle surplus inventory. You can choose to keep the surplus, distribute according to the forecast within the demand horizon, or distribute until all demand has been met. This is a good tool to use for overstock sales.

DEPLOYMENT HORIZON—This is the demand horizon to be considered when implementing a push distribution.

7.5.4 Storage location MRP

Please take note that this information set will only be displayed if you are maintaining MRP storage locations. You can define special procurement types, reorder points, and replenishment quantities specific to a storage location that you want to specially plan for in the MRP run.

7.6 Forecasting screen

The FORECASTING screen (see Figure 7.17) should only be created for a material if you are in a production environment that requires forecasting. For example, most make-to-stock companies produce inventory to a forecast, whereas make-to-order companies might prefer to use SAP's long-term planning functions rather than forecasting.

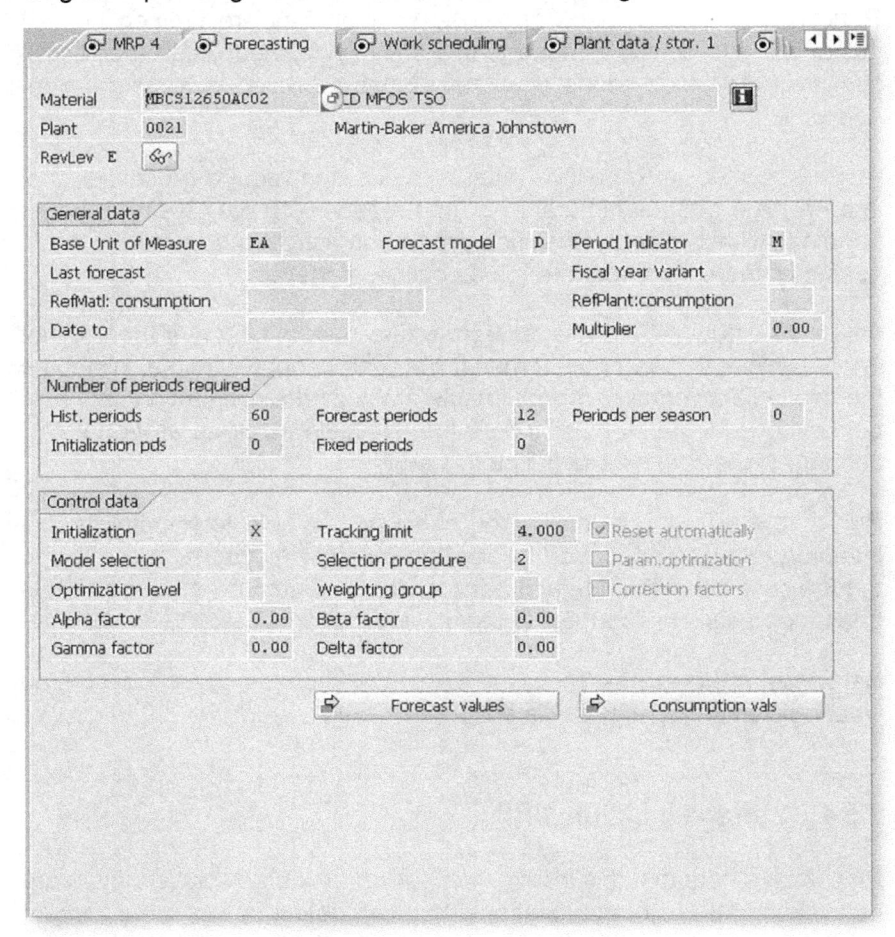

Figure 7.17: Forecasting screen

This screen contains three information sets: GENERAL DATA, NUMBER OF PERIODS REQUIRED, and CONTROL DATA. The fields within the GENERAL DATA information set are for basic information required to perform a forecast. The NUMBER OF PERIODS REQUIRED information set will define the scope of your forecast. The CONTROL DATA fields will determine how the forecast is calculated.

7.6.1 General data

BASE UNIT OF MEASURE—This is the same field that was previously defined in Chapter 4. It has been included here as a reference for forecasting. For more information, see Section 4.2.1.

FORECAST MODEL—In this field, you will select the type of forecasting you want to engage in. You have many choices. Some examples are constant model, seasonal, and moving average. The type you choose will depend on the kind of product you are forecasting.

PERIOD indicator—This field was previously defined in the MRP 3 screen. For more information, see Section 7.4.1. It has been included here for its reference to forecasting.

LAST FORECAST—This field will display the date of the last executed forecast.

FISCAL YEAR VARIANT—This field was previously defined in the MRP 3 screen. For more information, see Section 7.4.1. It has been included here for its reference to forecasting.

REFERENCE MATERIAL FOR CONSUMPTION—If you are creating a new material, you must reference another similar material in this field so that the system has historical consumption data, as the new material will not have any records.

REFERENCE PLANT FOR CONSUMPTION—Use this field to determine which plant the reference material's consumption data should be based upon.

DATE TO—This is used to decide how long you will use the reference material's consumption data for forecasting of your newly created material.

MULTIPLIER—Use this field to specify how much of the reference material's consumption data should be used to forecast your new material. The value is entered as a percentage in decimal format.

7.6.2 Number of periods required

HISTORICAL PERIODS—You can enter the number of previous periods to be used in the forecast calculation here.

FORECAST PERIODS—This is the number of periods in the future that you want to forecast.

PERIODS PER SEASON—This field is only used in seasonal forecasting models to inform the system how many periods to include in the season.

INITIALIZATION PERIODS—The value you enter here will govern how many periods are analyzed during the initial forecast.

FIXED PERIODS—This field is used to install what planners refer to as a frozen zone in the planning horizon. The forecast will not be recalculated for the number of periods defined in this field. This is used to help solidify capacity planning in the short term.

7.6.3 Control data

INITIALIZATION indicator—This indicator should be set as active prior to running the first forecast. It is used to determine certain parameters like trend values if you select automatic initialization. Alternatively, you can choose to manually define your beginning parameters during initialization.

TRACKING LIMIT—The value you set here is compared with the internally calculated tracking signal. If the difference between the tracking signals is greater than the tracking limit, you are issued an exception message to evaluate the forecast. This is an indication that your forecast has more deviation from actual requirements than you had expected.

RESET FORECAST MODEL AUTOMATICALLY indicator—By selecting this indicator as active, you are telling the system to reset the forecast model if you have exceeded the tracking limit.

MODEL SELECTION—In this field, you can choose to evaluate trend fluctuations, seasonal fluctuations, or both. This is used for automatic forecast model selection.

SELECTION PROCEDURE—This is another field used for automatic forecast model selection. You can either allow the system to choose between trend and seasonal, or you can have the system pick from all available models based on the mean absolute deviation from historical values. The latter is more time consuming, but more accurate.

PARAMETER OPTIMIZATION indicator—Set this field as active to automatically smooth parameters based on the forecast.

OPTIMIZATION LEVEL—This field will allow you to choose how much automatic smoothing should take place.

WEIGHT GROUP—This field is used to define how much weight should be placed on historical values in forecasting.

ALPHA FACTOR—The percentage you enter here in decimal format decides how much smoothing occurs for your basic value.

BETA FACTOR—The percentage you enter here in decimal format decides how much smoothing occurs for your trend value.

GAMMA FACTOR—The percentage you enter here in decimal format decides how much smoothing occurs for your seasonal index.

DELTA FACTOR—The percentage you enter here in decimal format decides how much smoothing occurs for your mean absolute deviation.

EXECUTE FORECAST icon—Click on this icon to manually execute a forecast.

7.7 Work scheduling screen

The WORK SCHEDULING screen (see Figure 7.18) contains information relevant to production. There are three information sets: GENERAL DATA, TOLERANCE DATA, and IN-HOUSE PRODUCTION TIME IN DAYS. The GENERAL DATA information set contains fields that specify how the material is treated in regard to its production area. The fields within the TOLERANCE DATA information set are used to restrict how much variance can occur between the original production order quantity and the final goods receipt. THE IN-HOUSE PRODUCTION TIME IN DAYS is a display of information used to calculate available capacity and guide scheduling procedures in the system.

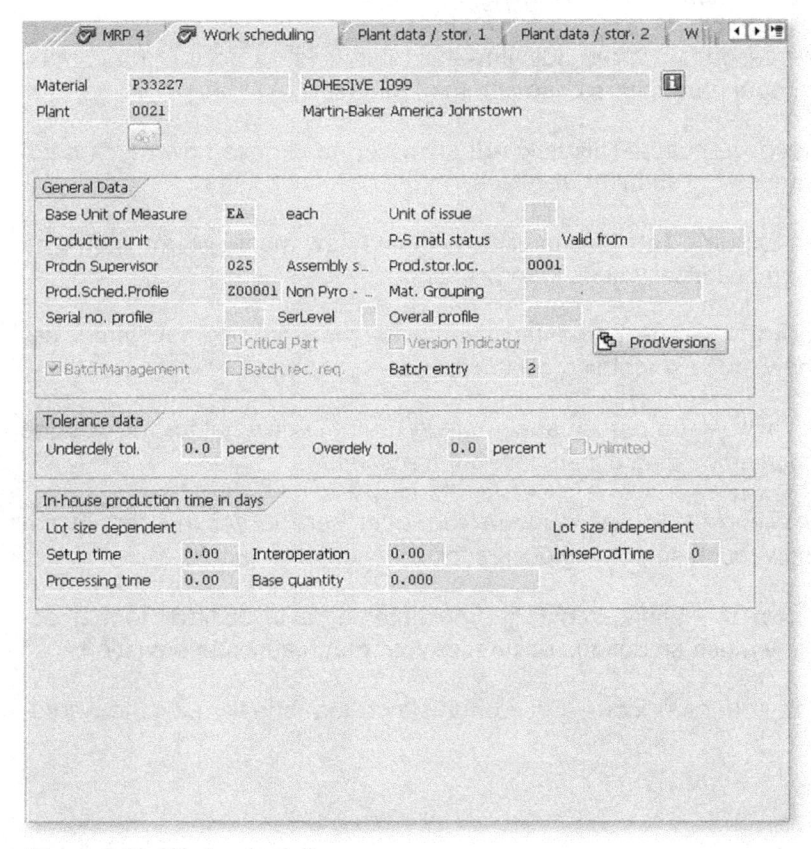

Figure 7.18: Work scheduling screen

7.7.1   General data

BASE UNIT OF MEASURE—This is the same field that was previously defined in Chapter 4. It has been included here as a reference for work scheduling. For more information, see Section 4.2.1.

UNIT OF ISSUE—As this title suggests, the unit of measure you enter here will be the unit in which the material is issued from the warehouse. The system uses its internal conversion factor table to convert the base unit of measure to the issuing unit of measure. This is useful when you are buying materials based on economies of scale and you want to consume those materials incrementally.

PRODUCTION UNIT—As this title suggests, the unit of measure you enter here will be the unit in which the material will be created upon the goods receipt of a production order. It is also dependent on the fact that you maintain the production unit in the routing. The system uses its internal conversion factor table to convert the base unit of measure to the production unit of measure. The system then checks to see if the production quantity falls within the specified lot size range.

PLANT SPECIFIC MATERIAL STATUS—This is the same field that was previously defined in Chapter 6. It has been included here as a reference for work scheduling. For more information, see Section 6.2.1.

VALID FROM—This is the same field that was previously defined in Chapter 6. It has been included here as a reference for work scheduling. For more information, see Section 6.2.1.

PRODUCTION SUPERVISOR—This field is used to assign a capacity planner to the material. There are capacity calculation settings in SAP customizing that can be tailored to each production supervisor.

PRODUCTION STORAGE LOCATION—This field was previously defined in this chapter. For more information, see Section 7.3.1

PRODUCTION SCHEDULING PROFILE—The profile that you assign in this field will govern your process for creating a production order. You can specify the timing of goods movements, automate production order printing, and specify how capacity is leveled amongst other choices. This profile can be very useful in eliminating wasteful administrative activities.

For instance, many organizations have no need to review a production order after it is released, but before it is printed. You can use this profile to allow automatic printing upon the release of an order.

MATERIAL GROUPING—You can use this field to group together materials that require the same operational setup. It is only useful for reporting features, as no systematic checks will take place.

SERIAL NUMBER PROFILE—This is the same field that was previously defined in Chapter 5. It has been included here as a reference for work scheduling. For more information, see Section 5.4.4.

SERIALIZATION LEVEL—This is the same field that was previously defined in Chapter 5. It has been included here as a reference for work scheduling. For more information, see Section 5.4.4.

OVERALL PROFILE—If you maintain this profile, you can individually control the change management process for sales orders, master data, and assembly orders for the given material. This will allow you to place more or less restriction on change authorization requirements.

CRITICAL PART indicator—This is the same field that was previously defined in Chapter 6. It has been included here as a reference for work scheduling. For more information, see Section 6.2.3.

VERSION indicator—This is the same field that was previously defined in this chapter. It has been included here as a reference for work scheduling. For more information, see Section 7.5.1.

BATCH MANAGEMENT indicator—This is the same field that was previously defined in Chapter 5. It has been included here as a reference for work scheduling. For more information, see Section 5.4.1.

APPROVED BATCH RECORD REQUIRED indicator—This is the same field that was previously defined in Chapter 5. It has been included here as a reference for work scheduling. For more information, see Section 5.4.1.

BATCH ENTRY—This is the same field that was previously defined in this chapter. It has been included here as a reference for work scheduling. For more information, see Section 7.3.1.

7.7.2 Tolerance data

UNDER DELIVERY TOLERANCE—In this plant-specific field you can express, by percentage, the amount of under delivery in goods receipt quantity you are willing to accept from the original production order quantity.

OVER DELIVERY TOLERANCE—In this plant-specific field you can express, by percentage, the amount of over delivery in goods receipt quantity you are willing to accept from the original production order quantity.

UNLIMITED DELIVERY indicator—Set this indicator to active if you are willing to accept an infinite number of over delivery from the original production order quantity.

7.7.3 In-house production time in days

By maintaining values in this field, you are using the alternative method to maintaining the in-house production time, as defined in Section 7.3.2. I personally recommend the following method because it more accurately describes the production process and has more uses in other business functions.

You can have the following fields updated in the material master by having the system evaluate the current production router. This is carried out by running SAP transactions CA96 followed by CA97 for the given material. Once this has been done, the MRP run will read the data stored in the following fields to perform scheduling activities. Combined together, the following fields consist of the in-house production time for the given material.

SETUP TIME—This field is the cumulative value, in work days, of all setup and tear down times within the current router. Setup and tear down are lot-size independent values.

INTEROPERATION TIME—This field is the cumulative value, in work days, of all move, queue, wait, float, and external processing times within the current router. These values are lot size independent.

IN-HOUSE PRODUCTION TIME—This is the same field that was previously defined in this chapter. For more information, see Section 7.3.2. This field has been included here for reference in the event you are not maintaining lot-size-dependent values.

PROCESSING TIME—This field is the cumulative value, in work days, of all direct labor or machine times within the current router. These values are lot-size dependent.

BASE QUANTITY—This is the quantity that the lot-size-dependent in-house production time is calculated on. This is particularly important in finite planning.

Use table reporting to develop your value stream for analysis

 If you are looking to set up the structure of a value stream for a particular product, you can get most of the necessary data from a single table report (SAP transaction SE16N). All of the planning information required to build a baseline value stream is contained in the in-house production time in the day's information set. By reporting on the table MARC and using your desired materials, you can gather the setup, interoperation, and processing time for all selected materials in one report. For more information on tables, see Section 2.1.

7.8 Personal experience

As a materials planner who uses SAP, I have found that there are two distinct obstacles to overcome in order to be successful. First of all, to use the full capabilities of the material master for effective planning, you must invest a large portion of time learning how the material master can be used to define your desired parameters. As you have seen in the length of this chapter, there are a number of subjects to understand before you can use the material master to your advantage. This can require formal education, help from professional consultants, and additional reading materials like this text. Personally, I have found that the best way to ensure comprehension is to develop my own theories and test them in a development client. If you are lucky enough to be part of an organization that will allow you to freely play around in an SAP development client, you will find it to be one of your greatest resources. If you do have access to one of these clients, you can try different scenarios and evaluate their outcomes for personal growth. I must caution you though. Just because you have proven to yourself that you can get a particular feature or setting to work does not mean that you should go ahead with implementation in the live system. You must be certain about what functions are impacted by any changes to the material master before proceeding. This may involve a bit of research with other functional areas.

Secondly, you must also understand the sales and operations process as it pertains to your plant and organization in order to decide where and when to implement your planning parameters. This involves understanding the unique capacity constraints, resource availability, procurement strategy, production strategy, core competencies, process capabilities, and other restrictions that will govern your material master settings. There may even be restrictions of a legal or environmental nature that will shape your planning parameters. The only way to gain this knowledge is to communicate with other functional silos in your organization. Get out on the shop floor and learn the production process from the assembler's perspective. Speak with those who procure your materials. Visit those who store and ship your products. Find out who enters sales orders and other requirements to see how they are entered. See what restrictions all of those individuals encounter so that you can tailor the material master to meet their needs. Finally, keep those lines of communication open. As your SAP skills mature, you may be able to enhance your plant's planning activities through the material master.

8 Inventory management

In this chapter, I will describe how the settings you make in the material master will determine how materials are stored and accounted for in SAP. Furthermore, I will discuss some of the specific put-away and picking procedures that are made available to you in the SAP Material Master.

I can tell you from personal experience that working in the stock room can be a thankless job. The level of multi-tasking required to perform this job is exceptional. First and foremost, in a production environment you must satisfy the ongoing demand of the shop floor. This can be difficult when there are several work centers simultaneously competing to fill their orders. Secondly, you must maintain constant cleanliness in order to protect valuable components and ensure workplace safety. A third important responsibility is inventory accuracy. If you are running a cycle count program of any significance, you are counting many materials each day. And if this isn't enough, you have to be concerned about inventory security. Those of us who have worked in a stock room know that materials have a way of "walking off" from time to time. When materials turn up missing, when production orders go unfilled, or when just about any material concern arises, it is the stock room personnel that take the heat.

While some of these issues can never completely be eliminated, I believe that the SAP Material Master offers some of the best inventory management solutions in existence today. These solutions were developed to automate routine functions and eliminate wasteful activities in material handling so that you can focus on what is important, filling orders timely and safely.

In this chapter, I will discuss the features of the material master that relate to inventory management from the stock room clerk's perspective. You will see how the material master's features will ensure that you keep expired inventory off your shelves, store inventory in proper locations, and use the appropriate tools and machines to get the job done.

8.1 Inventory management in the material master

Inventory management is about repetition. If you can find a way to reduce effort and wasteful activities in your repetitious operations, you will find that your time is better utilized. The material master offers a sound cycle counting process, built-in stock removal and placement procedures, as well as effective inventory control methods that will help your stock room reach its fullest potential.

Each stock room or warehouse is unique, so understanding the capabilities of the SAP Material Master will help you to tailor the settings within the following screens to meet your specific needs. There are four screens pertaining to inventory management. They are: PLANT DATA / STORAGE 1, PLANT DATA / STORAGE 2, WAREHOUSE MANAGEMENT 1, and WAREHOUSE MANAGEMENT 2.

8.2 Plant data / storage 1

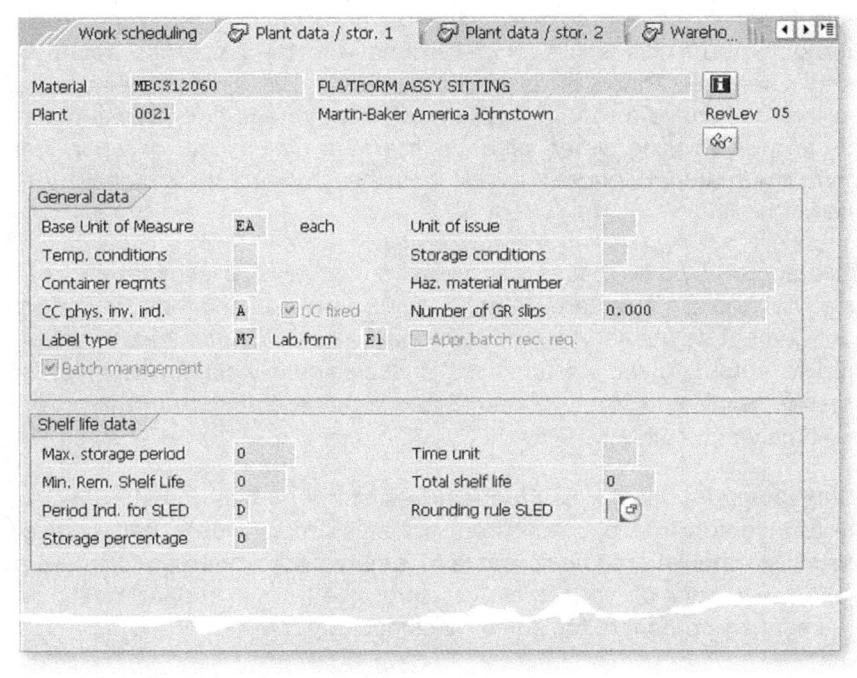

Figure 8.1: Plant data / storage 1 screen

The PLANT DATA / STORAGE 1 screen (see Figure 8.1) contains two information sets: GENERAL DATA and SHELF LIFE DATA. The fields within the general data information set control important features like required storage temperatures and characteristics for your cycle count process. The shelf life data information set contains the necessary information to control inventory that has an expiration date.

8.2.1 General data

BASE UNIT OF MEASURE—This is the same field that was defined in Chapter 4. For more information, see Section 4.2.1. I have incorporated here for reference for the conversion to the unit of issue.

UNIT OF ISSUE—This field was previously defined in Chapter 7. For more information, see Section 7.7.1. It has been included here for its relevance to selecting components for production.

Align your unit of issue to your production lot size

Defining the unit of issue can be a great opportunity for you to cut down on material handling time. Let's say, for example, that your base unit of measure is each (EA) for a particular bolt. It is a production process requirement to receive those bolts in sealed bags containing 120 bolts. Therefore, your buyer has convinced the bolt supplier to send the bolts in large quantities with 120 per bag. To consolidate the bolts down to one issuing unit, you can enter the unit bag (BAG) into the unit of issue field. This will present you with a conversion factor screen (see Figure 8.2) where you can enter the values 120 (EA) = 1 (BAG). Now, your pick list can call for 1 bag of bolts on each production order.

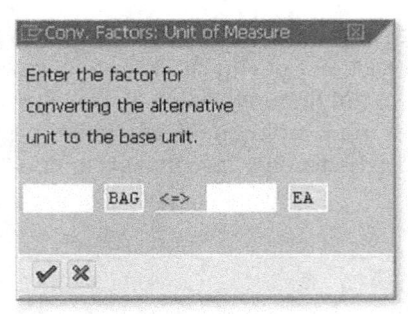

Figure 8.2: Conversion factor

The following four fields can be used for information only. However, with some slick customizing, you can incorporate this data on your receiving labels, which you can set up to print upon each goods receipt. This way, all of the necessary storage information is communicated to stock room personnel.

TEMPERATURE CONDITIONS indicator—In this field, you can enter a temperature condition, which must be specified in SAP customizing. It is for information only, but you can control where the item will be stored by creating a storage condition in the next field.

STORAGE CONDITIONS—In this field, you can specify a storage condition, which can be used to assign a particular storage location. For instance, if you must have an item temperature controlled, you can enter a storage condition that requires the item to be sent to a refrigerator that has been assigned for that storage condition.

CONTAINER REQUIREMENTS—This field will allow you to assign container types for storage and shipment, which must be defined in SAP customizing.

HAZARDOUS MATERIAL NUMBER—You can create hazardous material numbers in SAP customizing that you can assign to materials in this field. The numbers you create can be assigned a description of the hazard.

CYCLE COUNT PHYSICAL INVENTORY indicator—If you are still performing full inventory counts on an annual or semi-annual basis, you really need to investigate this section. Cycle counting is the most effective way to reduce inventory discrepancies by performing counts on a small segment of your inventory each day. This way, you are not forced to shut down your entire stock room for several days each year to perform counts. Additionally, because you are counting more frequently, you will be able to identify and correct inventory errors before too much time has passed and the error either grows, or its cause is forgotten. Furthermore, the cycle count process allows you to place emphasis on components that are more meaningful to your organization by counting them more frequently, while counting the less important items less frequently.

As I described in Chapter 7, ABC analysis allows you to place more emphasis on materials that are important to your organization (see Section 7.2.1). The cycle count indicator works on the same principle. As a matter of fact, you can assign the same ABC indicator value to the cycle count physical inventory indicator to govern how often a material is counted. However, you may have a motive to analyze materials for one significant factor in ABC analysis, for example, price, while analyzing the same material in a different capacity for cycle counting. For instance, importance to the production process might be a more appropriate factor for cycle counting. For this reason, the ABC ANALYSIS indicator and the CYCLE COUNT PHYSICAL INVENTORY indicator can have different settings for the same material.

CYCLE COUNT FIXED indicator—By setting this indicator to active, you are prohibiting those who perform the counts from adjusting the ABC ANALYSIS VALUE FOR CYCLE COUNT PHYSICAL INVENTORY indicator. Once this indicator is set, the CYCLE COUNT PHYSICAL INVENTORY indicator can only be changed by those who can maintain a material master record.

NUMBER OF GOODS RECEIPT SLIPS—The number you enter into this field will be the number of goods receipt documents or labels that will be printed upon each goods receipt of the item.

Case example: Number of goods receipt slips

 A consumer goods distributor ships shaving cream by the pallet (order unit PAL) containing 36 trays of shaving cream bottles per pallet. The receiving retail center must break apart each pallet upon receipt and distribute the shaving cream by tray for sale. Furthermore, in order for the retailers to distribute the trays of shaving cream from their inventory, each tray must be accompanied by a goods issue slip containing both part number and batch number. The distributer can easily automate this process by inserting the number 36 into the number of goods receipt slips field. Now, when a goods issue is created at the distributer for one pallet, 36 slips are printed and sent with the pallet to the retailer.

LABEL TYPE—If you want labels to print automatically upon certain goods movements, you must maintain a label type in this field. The label type can define which goods movements will trigger a printed label. The label type can also be used to determine which printer is used to generate the labels and how many will be printed. In order to print labels, you must also maintain the label form field.

LABEL FORM—This field is used to specify the type of label to print and the specific material information that will be printed on the label.

Use automatic label printing for your barcode readers

 If you are in a fast-paced or high-volume environment, I recommend creating your label form to include barcode format for information that is required for data entry later in your production process. For instance, if assembly technicians are required to enter batch numbers into the work order for backflushing as they consume component materials, it is wise to provide those technicians with barcode readers. By having your batch numbers printed out in barcode format on the goods receipt label and applying the label to the component material's storage container, the technician can simply scan the barcode to enter the batch number into the work order. This will decrease the data entry time, as well as eliminate typographical errors from the process.

APPROVED BATCH RECORD REQUIRED indicator—This field was previously defined in Chapter 5. For more information, see Section 5.4.1. It has been included here for its relevance to picking components for production. For example, if this indicator is activated, you will not be allowed to issue components to a production or process order if your batch record is not an approved format.

BATCH MANAGEMENT indicator—This field was previously defined in Chapter 5. For more information, see Section 5.4.1. It has been included here for its relevance to picking components for production. Maintaining batch management is a requirement for cycle counting.

8.2.2   Shelf life data

MAXIMUM STORAGE PERIOD—In this plant-specific field, you can enter the maximum amount of time that a material should be kept in inventory. The value you enter here is according the unit of time defined in the time unit field. This field is for information only and has no link to automatic shelf life procedures that are internal to SAP.

TIME UNIT—The unit of time used to define the maximum storage period.

MINIMUM REMAINING SHELF LIFE—The value that you enter in this globally maintained field will be used in a system check upon goods receipt. If you specify a value here, there must be at least that amount of shelf life remaining on the material in order to process a goods receipt. If there is not, you will be presented with an exception error or warning. The unit of time applied to this value is specified in the PERIOD indicator for SHELF LIFE EXPIRATION DATE field.

If you are using materials that expire, maintaining this field is a necessity to proper inventory management. The amount of required remaining shelf life may depend on government law, industry standards, or simply the amount of risk you are willing to accept from having an item expire on your shelf.

TOTAL SHELF LIFE—As the title suggests, the value that you enter in this globally maintained field will be used by the system to calculate the final shelf expiration date of the material. Upon goods receipt, you will be required to enter the date of production of the material. The system adds the value entered in the TOTAL SHELF LIFE field to the production date to calculate the shelf expiration date. This information can then be applied to a shelf life expiration report, which will inform inventory control personnel when to remove items from the shelf by batch.

PERIOD INDICATOR FOR SHELF LIFE EXPIRATION DATE—The unit of time applied to the values entered in the shelf life fields.

ROUNDING RULE FOR SHELF LIFE EXPIRATION DATE—If you are using a period indicator that is larger than day (D), such as week (W) or year (Y), you can define if the expiration date should be rounded to the beginning or to the end of the defined period when calculated from the production date.

For example, you entered a date of production for a material as March 17th and the item has a six-month shelf life. You are using the period indicator month (M) and you set your rounding profile to the end of the chosen period (+). The expiration date of the material will be calculated as August 31st, the last day of the period in which the actual calculated date falls.

STORAGE PERCENTAGE—The value you enter here, as a percentage, will be the amount of time that must be available in the remaining shelf life in order to ship it to a customer or another plant.

This field can be valuable when customers define how much shelf life must remain on an item before they will accept it into inventory. I have found it to be extremely useful in selling items to the U.S. Government, where remaining shelf life is specifically defined and violations of the shelf life requirement can bring on expensive customer rejections and corrective actions.

8.3   Plant data / storage 2 screen

The PLANT DATA / STORAGE 2 screen (see Figure 8.3) contains two information sets: WEIGHT / VOLUME and GENERAL PLANT PARAMETERS. Most of the fields within each of these information sets have already been defined in previous screens. They are referenced again here to group together all of the necessary data required for proper storage in the warehouse. This way, those who work in inventory management have all of their pertinent information in one place.

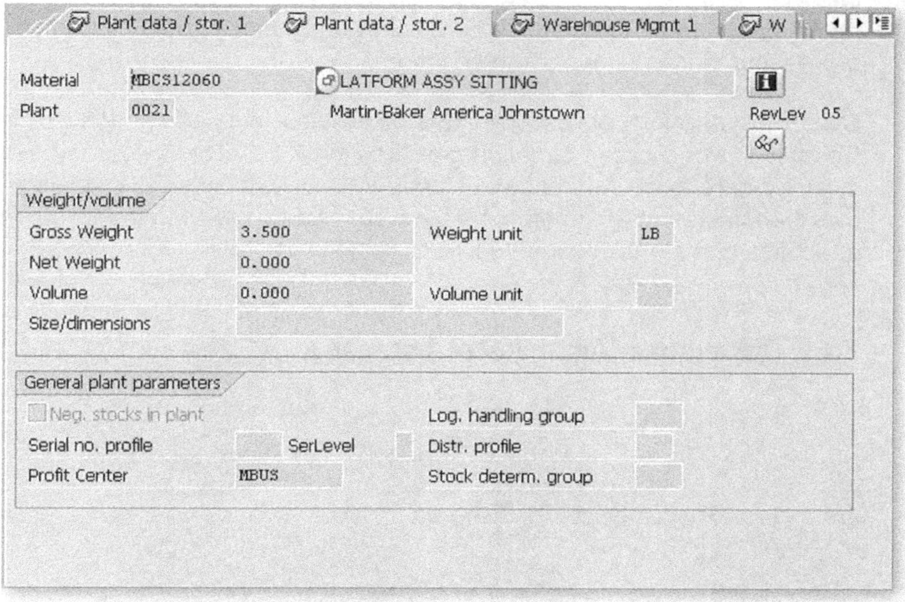

Figure 8.3: Plant data / storage 2 screen

8.3.1 Weight / volume

All of the fields in this information set have been previously defined in Chapter 4. For more information, see Section 4.2.3. These fields have been included here for their relevance to warehouse management. The weights and volumes of each item can be used to project required storage space and automate material put-away activities.

8.3.2 General plant parameters

With the exception of two fields, LOGISTICS HANDLING GROUP and STOCK DETERMINATION GROUP, all of the fields in this information set have been previously defined in Chapter 5. For more information, see Section 5.4.4. These fields have been included here due to their relevance to detailed inventory information.

LOGISTICS HANDLING GROUP—You can use this field to group together similar materials for the purpose of put-away and picking functions. For instance, you may want to create a group called "liquids" to be able to report on all items that require containers that handle liquids when you are issuing those materials to production.

STOCK DETERMINATION GROUP—This field was previously defined in Chapter 7. For more information, see Section 7.3.1. This field has been included here for its reference to storing inventory. It is useful in a repetitive manufacturing environment where specific put-away rules for large quantities of material must be defined.

8.4   Warehouse Management 1 screen

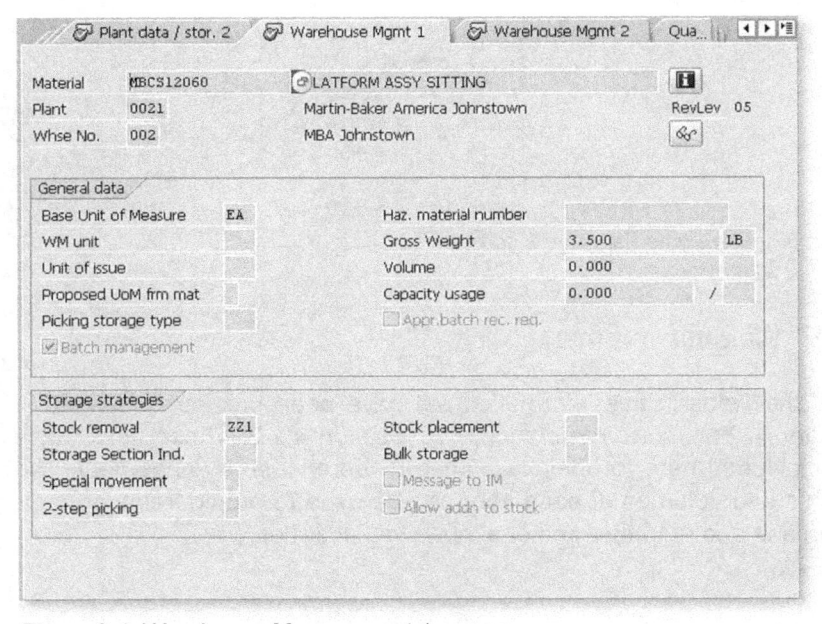

Figure 8.4: Warehouse Management 1 screen

The WAREHOUSE MANAGEMENT 1 screen (see Figure 8.4) contains two information sets: GENERAL DATA and STORAGE STRATEGIES. Both information sets contain fields pertaining to how materials are issued from the warehouse and fields that will guide the put-away process. The choices you make in these fields will help you to eliminate wasteful material handling activities if properly maintained. Again, many of these fields have been previously defined but are collected here to aid inventory management personnel in their picking and put-away tasks.

8.4.1 General data

BASE UNIT OF MEASURE—This is the same field that was defined in Chapter 4. For more information, see Section 4.2.1. It has been incorporated here for reference for the conversion to the unit of issue and warehouse management unit of measure.

HAZARDOUS MATERIAL NUMBER—This field was previously defined in this chapter. For more information, see Section 8.2.1.

WAREHOUSE MANAGEMENT UNIT OF MEASURE—This plant-specific field is another alternate unit of measure. It can be used just like any other alternate unit of measure, where a conversion factor must be maintained if an entry is made in this field. It is used for inventory purposes only.

Case example: Warehouse management unit of measure

The Smooth Move Lubricant Corporation sells bottles of aerosol lubricants to many customers across the globe in various sizes. In order to match large and fluctuating demand of each bottle size, they must maintain a very large inventory of bottles. The new supply manager insists on a highly accurate inventory system, which requires a significant cycle count program. The problem is that the base unit of measure for the corporation is each (EA). This means that, according to the cycle count process, the count must be performed per bottle. However, the inventory clerk has been in the industry for a while. She knows that bottles are stored on pallets, and that each pallet holds a certain number of bottles. The pallets are never broken down until after they have been issued from the warehouse. The inventory clerk uses this knowledge and SAP's capabilities to her advantage by maintaining the warehouse unit of measure pallet (PAL) along with the appropriate conversion factor. This allows the inventory clerk to make her cycle counts by the pallet, thereby significantly reducing the time it takes for a daily cycle count.

GROSS WEIGHT—This field was previously defined in Chapter 4. For more information, see Section 4.2.3. It has been included here for reference to warehouse management.

UNIT OF ISSUE—This field was previously defined in Chapter 7. For more information, see Section 7.7.1. It has been included here for reference to warehouse management.

VOLUME—This field was previously defined in Chapter 4. For more information, see Section 4.2.3. It has been included here for reference to warehouse management.

PROPOSED UNIT OF MEASURE FROM MATERIAL MASTER—Maintain a value in this field if you want the system to propose a specific unit of measure that differs from the base unit of measure in SAP inventory transactions. This can be helpful if you have several alternate units of measure for a given material, but you have a preference for a particular one and want it to be proposed to other users when processing inventory transactions.

CAPACITY USAGE—You can use this field to specify how much of the storage capacity is used by each procurement unit. This can help you to manage storage in finite spaces.

PICKING STORAGE TYPE—The field storage type was previously defined in Chapter 2. For more information, see Section 2.2.1. The picking storage type is the type of storage that you want to use in planning your storage capacity.

APPROVED BATCH RECORD REQUIRED indicator—This field was previously defined in Chapter 5. For more information, see Section 5.4.1. It has been included here for reference to warehouse management.

BATCH MANAGEMENT indicator—This field was previously defined in Chapter 5. For more information, see Section 5.4.1. It has been included here for reference to warehouse management.

8.4.2 Storage strategies

STORAGE TYPE INDICATOR FOR STOCK REMOVAL—In this field, you can define, in hierarchal order, the storage type from which stock is removed during the picking process. This can be helpful in reducing material handling. For instance, if you've used up all inventory in the normal production storage location, where pallets are broken down into individual units, you can dictate that the next storage location to be used for picking is another similar storage location within the plant containing individual units before proceeding to the location where bulk storage occurs in full pallets.

STORAGE TYPE INDICATOR FOR STOCK PLACEMENT—This field works in the same way as the storage type indicator for stock removal, but as the title suggests, this field is for stock placement.

STORAGE SECTION indicators—This field also works like the two previous fields, but instead of considering the preference of storage type, the entry you make in this field will consider the section of the warehouse. SAP storage bins can be classified into storage sections within the warehouse. The storage section is a physical location used for each storage type.

BULK STORAGE indicators—If you are storing materials in bulk, you can define bulk storage indicators in SAP customizing to spell out how many units can be stacked or placed on a rack.

SPECIAL MOVEMENT INDICATOR FOR WAREHOUSE MANAGEMENT—You can use this field to direct a given material to a storage type that differs from the general rules of your goods movements. For instance, if your goods movement for receipt generally puts all materials into the storage type XYZ, but you wish for the given material to be sent to a more secure location upon receipt, you can enter a special movement indicator that will send the material to the alternate storage type ABC. Maintaining this field can help reduce material handling by placing the item into the appropriate storage type automatically rather than having to transfer it after receipt.

MESSAGE TO INVENTORY MANAGEMENT indicator—If activated, you can use this field to send defined warehouse management data to inventory management personnel in other locations automatically.

2-STEP PICKING—By maintaining this field, you are saying that you want to use a two-step picking process to reduce material handling transactions when picking several orders. For instance, if 2-step picking is activated for a material and you have several deliveries to process, the system will ask you to pick the entire amount required for all deliveries in the first step, and then pick each individual delivery quantity in the second step. This keeps the material handler from having to go back to the original storage location for each delivery.

ALLOWANCE FOR ADDITIONAL STOCK indicator—If you activate this indicator, you will be allowed to add additional stock of the same material to a storage bin already containing that material. Otherwise, only one batch of material is allowed in each storage bin.

If it is critical that you trace your components by batch, I recommend that you do not allow additional stock in your storage bins. The chance of mixing batch numbers and losing valuable batch traceability will be significantly increased by allowing the additional stock.

8.5 Warehouse Management 2 screen

The WAREHOUSE MANAGEMENT 2 screen (see Figure 8.5) contains only one information set, which is PALLETIZATION DATA. The fields within this information set are used to propose the number of loading units required to store a given material.

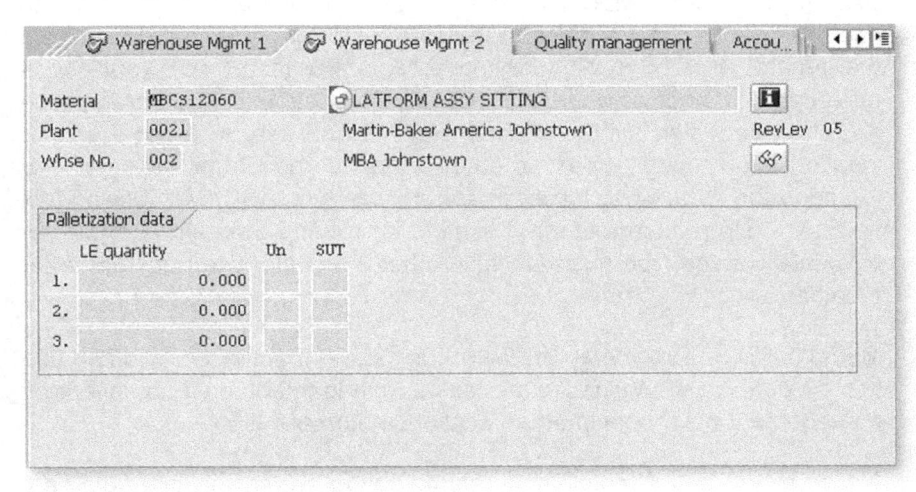

Figure 8.5: Warehouse Management 2 screen

8.5.1 Palletization data

The next three fields work together to propose how the material should be packed for loading into storage. For example, if you have 40 bottles of gas that need to be placed into stock, and your forklift can only lift 10 bottles at a time on a wooden pallet, you would choose your loading equipment quantity to be 10. You would choose your loading equipment unit of measure to be bottle (BT). Additionally, you would choose your storage unit type to be pallet (PAL). Now the system will propose that you use 4 pallets to store your batch of 40 bottles.

LOADING EQUIPMENT QUANTITY—The quantity you enter here is the quantity that will fit on one storage unit.

UNIT OF MEASURE FOR LOADING EQUIPMENT—This is the unit in which the loading equipment quantity is measured. It is used for conversion to the storage unit type.

STORAGE UNIT TYPE—The selection you make in this field defines the storage unit container. In the example above, the storage unit type is pallet.

8.6 Personal experience

My personal experience of working as a stockroom clerk was an educational one. As a learning experience, I was fortunate enough to work in the stock room during a very transitional time. It was a time of significant growth in sales and staffing for our company. The increase in our sales put a lot of pressure on our stock room, which caused our inventory management activities to gain the attention and focus of senior leadership.

We had two significant problems at the time. The first problem was that we were routinely unpleasantly surprised by stock outs due to incorrect inventory quantities. The second issue was that I was the only employee in the stock room at the time, which made it very difficult to keep up with the growing production floor demand. At the time, the stock room was viewed by many as one of the main roadblocks to an acceptable customer satisfaction rate. Fortunately, we soon implemented SAP, the software whose tools offered the solutions we needed to get through our barriers to success.

The stock-out problem was a direct effect of our inventory reconciliation process. At that time, our company would take an annual inventory count to reconcile discrepancies. We would shut down production for two to three days every year and several employees would volunteer to perform the counts. There were many faults with this process. One fault was that many of the volunteers performing the counts were not familiar with all parts, locations, storage bins. This resulted in a lot of chaos in our small storage space. Bins were confused and mixed together. The volunteers also occasionally returned bins to the wrong storage location after counting. The second fault was that some of the personnel who volunteered to perform the counts were simply looking for a diversion from their daily work. Therefore, their counts were often lackadaisical and incorrect. These issues added to the overall problem of inventory errors not being addressed in a timely manner. When you only count inventory once or twice a year, you will have no chance at reconciling errors that may have occurred months ago, the cause of which is buried in thousands of inventory transactions and furthered by erroneous reconciliation counts. From time to time this would amount to us showing more inventory in SAP than we physically had, and thereby causing a stock out.

We knew we needed to stop the vicious cycle of inventory errors and lack of corrections. So, shortly after I left my stock room duties, we implemented SAP's cycle count process. We now had controlled daily counts according to our ABC analysis. This meant that inventory was being counted by a trained inventory professional and reconciled immediately by an independent verifier who was also very familiar with our picking and storage process. By having inventory errors addressed in a timely manner, we began to regain control of our inventory because we could more easily identify the root of the problem.

The second problem, filling the demand of the production floor, was also addressed by SAP's warehouse management system. A problem with our legacy system was that the storage locations were not defined in enough detail. This would cause us to store inventory for similar products in physically diverse storage locations, which made the picking process longer than it needed to be. We now had a system to better classify those storage locations. With SAP's warehouse management capabilities, we began to store items commonly used in the same production process in the same inventory location. This sped up the picking process tremendously. In hindsight, had I also implemented some of the material groupings offered in the material master to classify how and where components were to be stored, we would have had even more control over the storage and picking process. As a result, I highly recommend using the picking and storage strategies available to you in the material master in a way that suits your particular organization's need for organization and detail. You will find a significant reduction in material handling and inventory reporting by doing so.

9 Quality management

In this chapter, I will describe the SAP Material Master settings that will define how a material is inspected for quality control. You will also find out how the material master can ensure that the given material is accompanied by any required quality conformance documentation.

So far, I've covered the material master from a logistics perspective. You've seen how different manufacturing environments plan their work. You've seen how sales are translated into requirements, and how requirements are grouped and satisfied by procurement and production activities. You have also seen how inventory is stored and checked for accuracy. These are the functions that allow any business to operate, but what I haven't covered is what makes your product desirable. The answer to that is the reliability in the performance of your product. In order to instill dependability in your product, you must have a mechanism of control that ensures process consistency and specification conformance throughout the procurement and production process.

In this chapter, I will cover the features available in the SAP Material Master that allow you to implement these necessary controls. To ensure that your organization's quality management system is implemented in SAP properly, I recommend that those who enter the quality control parameters into the material master are the same individuals who create the inspection profiles used for procurement and production. This is often a quality planner; an individual trained in blue print interpretation, quality inspection, and quality management planning. By assigning the quality management segment of the material master to the quality planner, you are giving that individual the vision of the entire quality assurance process within SAP. This way, the quality planner will know how his or her inspection plan is linked to the procurement and production process. This is particularly important in an ISO-certified environment, where a proven and robust quality system is required and systematic functions must be fully comprehended by the appropriate stakeholders.

9.1 Quality management structure in the material master

There is only one material master screen for quality assurance; the QUALITY MANAGEMENT screen. In most environments, every material procured or produced will have acceptance criteria of some type. This screen is used to assign those necessary inspection types and profiles to a given material. It is also used to define what documents and certifications might be necessary to procure a material. Once the links between the material and the inspection profiles are set up, the inspection criteria will be imbedded into production orders as specified in the router operations and in purchase orders for inspection prior to goods receipt.

9.2 Quality management screen

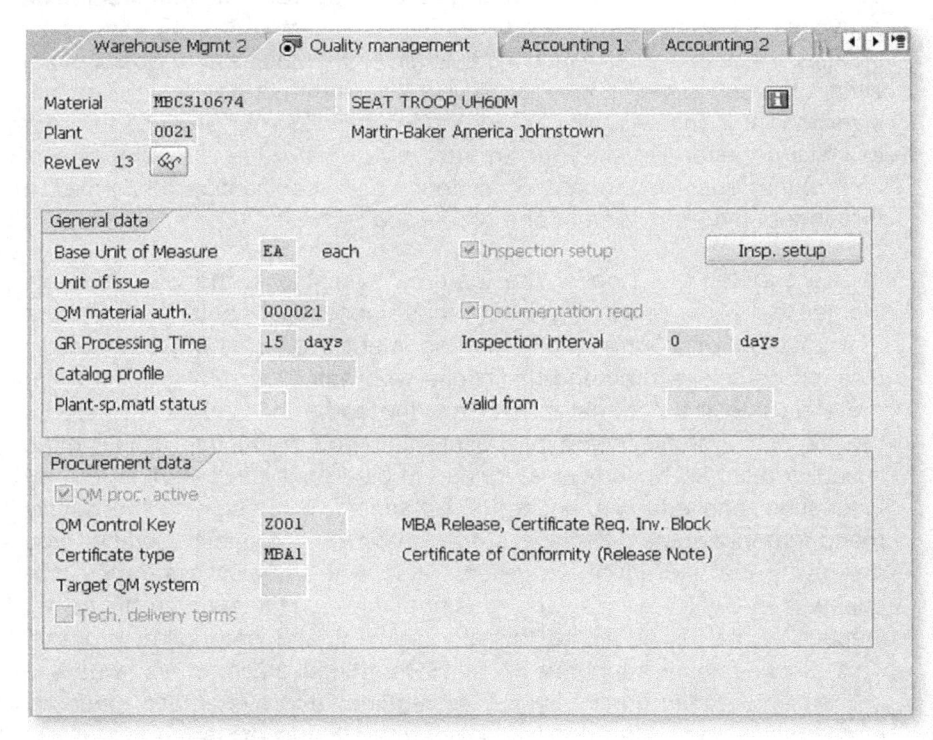

Figure 9.1: Quality management screen

The QUALITY MANAGEMENT screen (see Figure 9.1) consists of two information sets: GENERAL DATA and PROCUREMENT DATA. Some of the fields contained in the GENERAL DATA section have been previously defined in other chapters, but are included here for their relevance to inspection lot calculations and MRP scheduling. Other fields within this information set are used to define the type of inspection required for the material. The fields within the PROCUREMENT DATA information set are mostly used to define what type of documentation is required in order to accept a procured item into inventory.

9.2.1 General data

BASE UNIT OF MEASURE—This is the same field that was defined in Chapter 4. For more information, see Section 4.2.1. It has been incorporated here for its relevance to quality management (QM) lot sizes.

QM lot sizes are the sample sizes that must be inspected of an entire batch of material according to the sampling lot size procedures that you define. These lot sample size procedures use the base unit of measure to perform the calculation.

INSPECTION SETUP EXISTS indicator—This indicator is set to active if you have created inspection data for the given material. It is simply a quick visual reference to let you know that inspection data exists, and it is not displayed on this screen. You can view the inspection data that has been set up by clicking on the INSPECTION SETUP icon.

INSPECTION SETUP icon—When you click on this icon, you will go to the INSPECTION SETUP DATA screen (see Figure 9.2) where you can create, change, or view inspection setup data for each inspection type that you desire. This is not the screen where you will create your specific inspection criteria for the material such as dimensional characteristics, rather the screen where you will define what production activities and goods movements allow and/or require inspections. You must maintain inspection setup data in the material master to link your inspection profiles to the production and procurement activities for the material.

Furthermore, for each inspection type that you define, you can maintain rules for that inspection type in the DETAILED INFORMATION ON INSPECTION TYPE information set within this screen (see Figure 9.2). In the screen

capture, you can see that inspection type (01) GOODS RECEIPT INSPEC-
TION FOR PURCHASE ORDERS has been activated. The rules of that inspection type are chosen in the DETAILED INFORMATION ON INSPECTION TYPE
information set below. Separate detailed information is available for each
inspection type that you have activated. The detailed information of each
can be displayed by clicking on the desired inspection type.

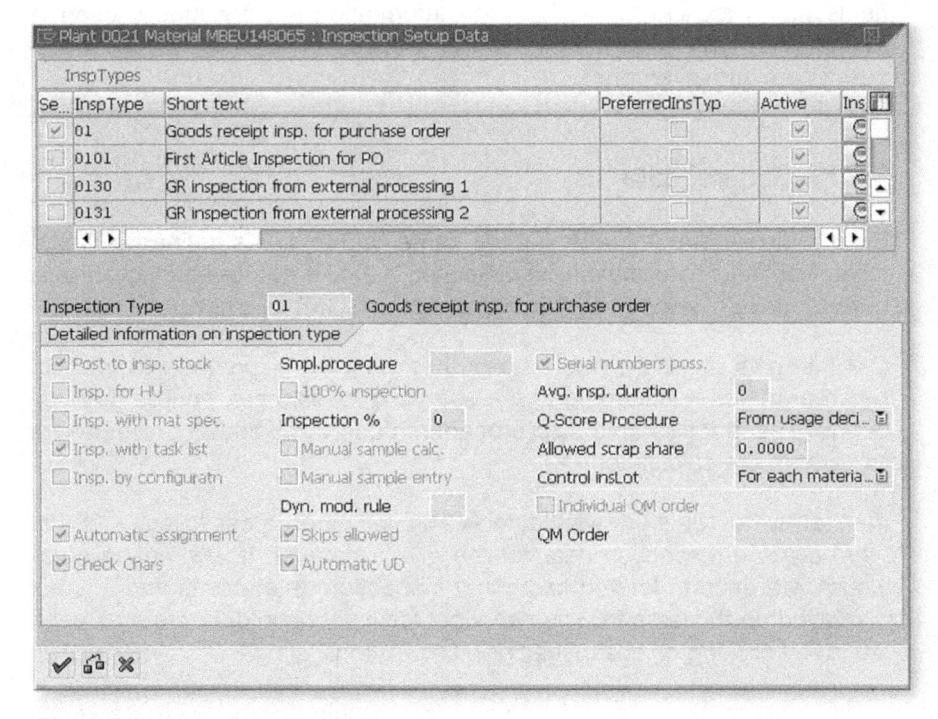

Figure 9.2: Inspection setup data screen

UNIT OF ISSUE—This field was previously defined in Chapter 7. For more
information, see Section 7.7.1. It has been included here for its relevance to QM lot sizes. If the unit of issue differs from the base unit of
measure, the sample lot size procedure will use the unit of issue to perform the calculation.

QM MATERIALS AUTHORIZATION GROUP—You can use this field to restrict
authorization to certain quality management functions by maintaining QM
authorization groups in SAP customizing. This is useful when you want
to ensure that only trained and qualified personnel enter or amend in-

spection criteria or the specific results recorded upon inspection. An important aspect of an inspection lot is the final acceptance, which SAP calls the usage decision. You can also restrict who has authorization to make the usage decision within this authorization group.

DOCUMENTATION REQUIRED indicator—The name of this field is slightly misleading. It is not an indicator stating that documentation is required to perform the inspection, but rather a requirement placed on SAP. If you set this indicator to active, you are saying that you want the system to document all changes made to inspection lots and usage decisions by means of a change document. A change document is simply a recorded history within the system of any given change. This can be useful in tracking down erroneous entries or to prove when an action occurred.

GOODS RECEIPT PROCESSING TIME—This field was previously discussed in Chapter 6. For more information, see Section 6.2.3. It has been included here for its relevance to the lead time for in house inspection after the item has been received.

INSPECTION INTERVAL—This field is used when several inspections are required at specified intervals. You can define the interval period in this field. For instance, in chemical production it may be necessary to inspect your product at specified intervals after the reaction has taken place.

CATALOG PROFILE—When a product is found to be non-conforming, a quality inspector can create a quality notification in the QM module. This notification will document the discrepancy of the product and capture all associated tasks to evaluate and correct the issue. Within the quality notification there are several different group codes that can be used to classify the discrepancy. This field can be used to restrict values of the available group codes in quality notifications for any given notification type that is applied to the material.

PLANT SPECIFIC MATERIAL STATUS—This is the same field that was previously defined in Chapter 6. It has been included here as a reference for quality planning. For more information, see Section 6.2.1. Quality planners may have reason to restrict the usage of a given material based on its quality characteristics. It may be prudent to have plant-specific material statuses created for quality planning purposes if they are necessary in your environment.

VALID FROM—This is the same field that was previously defined in Chapter 6. It has been included here as a reference for quality planning. For more information, see Section 6.2.1.

9.2.2 Procurement data

QM IN PROCUREMENT indicator—By setting this indicator to active, you are saying that you want to maintain QM procurement procedures for all plants in the organization. You must further define the QM procurement requirements of each plant by maintaining a QM control key for each plant.

QM CONTROL KEY—If you are requiring inspections for your procured materials by setting the QM IN PROCUREMENT indicator to active, you must define the attributes of your quality requirements in control keys. You will select the appropriate control key for each plant in this field.

CERTIFICATE TYPE—You can use this field to select the type of certificate that you either require for the procurement of the material or that you want to issue upon sale of the material. The attributes of the certificate type can be defined in SAP customizing.

TARGET QM SYSTEM—When procuring an item from a vendor, the system will check the QM systems stored in the vendor master against the desired QM system stored in the material master. If there is no match, the system will issue a warning to state that you are procuring a material from a vendor with a quality system that differs from the target QM system for the material. This is useful, for instance, if you need to ensure that all products are procured from vendors with a certain level of ISO certification.

TECHNICAL DELIVERY TERMS EXIST indicator—If you have defined technical delivery terms for the given material in your plant within document management, this indicator will be set to active. This is an indication that technical delivery terms can or will be printed upon PO creation.

Develop a cross-functional inspection planning process

 I recommend that you develop a documented planning process that includes quality planners, production planners, and buyers for inspection plan implementation. If you have a procedure in place that details how and when inspection plans are to be created and implemented into production routers and purchase orders, you will save yourself a lot of headaches down the road. It may be helpful to have a team meeting when developing new routers and procuring new materials so that inspection plans are conducive to the flow of production, while still capturing all of the necessary inspection criteria. From a quality planner's perspective, there should be an inspection operation between each small step in the production process. From a production planner's perspective, there should be as little interruption to the production process as possible. It is the responsibility of both planner types to work together to find a router/inspection plan that meets the needs of both schools of thought. It is much easier to form this plan upfront rather than try to amend an inspection plan in a work order once it has been released to production.

9.3 Personal experience

In my production environment, quality assurance is at the forefront of our operations. The aerospace industry is completely reliant on sound quality management systems that are held to the highest ISO standards. Therefore, we require our ERP system to control product flow through incremental steps of acceptance through our quality system. From an operations management perspective, it can be painful at times to work under such scrutiny because the entire production process can come to a halt due to something as simple as a typo on a material certification. However, when I look at the big picture of the items we are producing, I am reminded that the safety of those flying in planes around the globe is dependent on the strict control of our quality systems. Fortunately, SAP offers the necessary means of control.

In the early days of our SAP implementation, we would find ourselves being issued corrective actions by our government quality assurance representatives (DCMA) because they would review the inspection data with an associated batch of material and find that not all inspection criteria was satisfied, but the batch of material was accepted into stock. While we were confident that our internal inspectors were doing their jobs appropriately, we could not prove that all inspection criteria had been satisfied. Whether the inspector had not performed the particular inspection, or they simply forgot to make the entry into the inspection profile was beside the point. We needed to ensure that all criteria were completed before the material was accepted into inventory.

After presenting this problem to our IT department, they offered an effective SAP solution. By simply defining the checking rules of the control keys in our production routers and the goods movement rules for our purchase order receipts in SAP customizing, we were able to install an error message that prevented further processing or goods movements when an inspector tried to complete their acceptance, but a characteristic was found to be incomplete. This error message essentially forced all characteristics to be complete without question. It was a simple fix, but a great example of the level of control offered by SAP.

10 Accounting

In this chapter, I will discuss how a given material is assigned financial value in SAP.

The backbone of every organization is its accounting system. The leaders of your organization most likely spend a good portion of their time using and reporting on the data generated from this system to make just about every critical and strategic decision pertaining to your company. Therefore, this data must be unquestionably reliable. In order to produce accurate and consistent accounting data that not only conforms to generally accepted accounting principles, but also provides meaningful information for this internal analysis, an organization must maintain comprehensive records of planned costs in a controlled environment. Those planned costs will be used by the organization's leadership to calculate the fiscal budget; the financial measuring stick for your company's operating costs. In your case, that controlled environment is the SAP Material Master.

The title of this chapter can be misleading. It is generally not an accountant that maintains the fields within the accounting screens; rather it is those who are closely related to the procurement and production process. Those individuals who create the planned costing data are generally very familiar with procurement techniques, preferred sources of supply, production techniques, production work centers, and BOM and routing data. Only those individuals, such as buyers, planners, and cost estimators have this intimate knowledge, and this chapter has been written from their perspective.

10.1 Accounting in the material master

The material master screens related to accounting are where the planned costs of every aspect of your production environment are collected. There are six screens of the material master pertaining to accounting functions: ACCOUNTING 1, ACCOUNTING 2, COSTING 1, COSTING 2, PLANT STOCK, and STORAGE LOCATION STOCK. The settings that you make within the first four screens will govern how and when to collect planned costs. After procurement, production and subsequent sales occur, it is those planned costs that will be used as the basis to determine what cost variances you've experienced and how profitable you've been. The latter two screens, PLANT STOCK and STORAGE LOCATION STOCK, can be used to report the overall status of the material quantities within inventory.

Because production and procurement techniques can vary from plant to plant, and tax rates will vary from region to region, nearly all of the fields within the following screens are plant specific. This way, costs and profitability will be calculated based on your plant's specific material, labor, and overhead rates.

Before making any entries into the following screens, it is important that you understand the difference between standard price and moving average price. You must also know which method of inventory valuation your organization is going to practice. The method that is chosen will most likely represent how all inventory is valued for your organization and it is a critical building block to all financial reporting and analysis.

If you are valuating a material at standard price, you either enter this price manually or automatically using a costing run. In production, the standard price then serves as a benchmark to compare the actual production costs to. By analyzing the variance between the standard price and the actual costs incurred in production, you can identify where your value chain is not operating as planned. Possible reasons for production variances could be, for example:

▶ Price changes to input materials

▶ Price changes to labor costs

▶ Quantity changes (increased or decreased consumption of components and/or labor, scrap)

On the other hand, the standard price can be used to determine the sales margin in your organization. If you measure your sales department on a contribution margin, the standard price defines the cost of goods sold. It cannot be influenced by the sales department anyway, so it's fair to set a fixed cost of goods sold rate for the entire year. The sales margin is then only dependent on the sales revenue, which is the sales department's task to impact.

The standard price will then remain constant until you update it. You will usually want to keep your standard price stable over the course of a year to give the sales department a reliable planning base. You should only recalculate the standard price if there is a major change in input prices (material or labor cost).

If you choose to valuate a material on moving average price, then the system will automatically adjust the price whenever you post a goods receipt for the material at a price different than the current moving average price.

Example: Valuation at moving average price

Let's assume the total inventory of a material is 100 pieces, at a moving average price of $10. The total stock value is therefore $1,000. If you then receive 10 pieces of the same material at a value of $12, the system valuates the additional stock at $120. The new total inventory value is then 1,000 + 120 = $1,120. The new moving average price is 1,120 / 110 = $10.18.

The advantage of valuating a material at moving average price is that the material is always valuated at the current market price.

Valuation strategy for material

SAP strongly recommends valuating all materials manufactured in-house (finished goods and semi-finished goods) at standard price. All items you purchase (raw materials, trading goods, etc.) should be valuated at moving average price.

10.2 Accounting 1 screen

The ACCOUNTING 1 screen (see Figure 10.1) has two information sets: GENERAL DATA and CURRENT VALUATION. The fields within the GENERAL DATA information set are used to define the basic framework of your standard calculations such as the currency you are working in and the division of the business that your financial costs will settle to. The fields within the CURRENT VALUATION information set will help to determine inventory values and where those inventory values are stored in the accounting ledger.

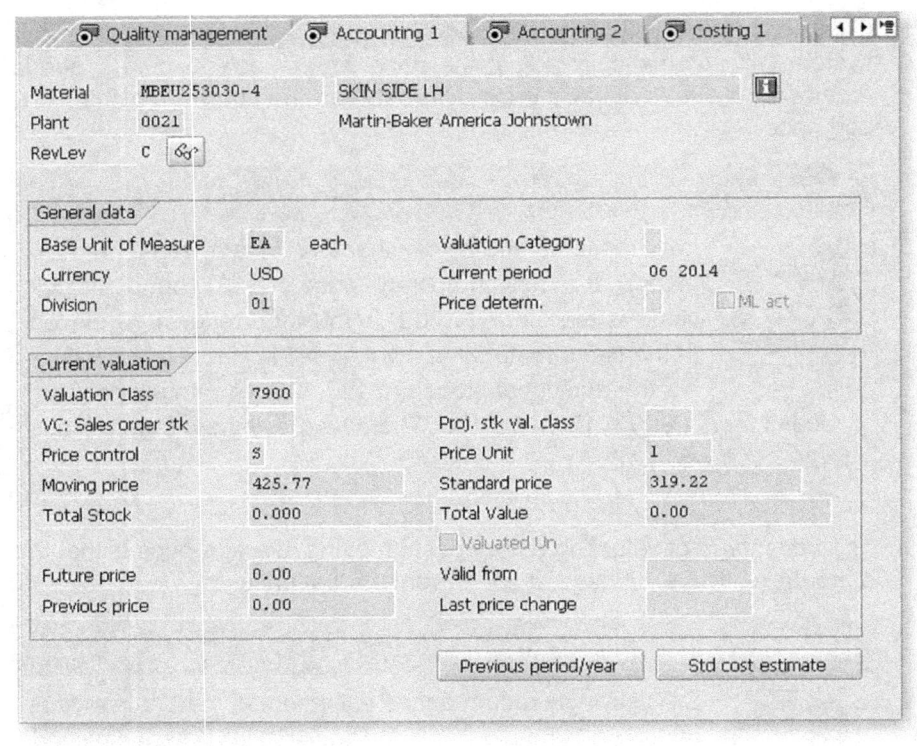

Figure 10.1: Accounting 1 screen

10.2.1 General data

BASE UNIT OF MEASURE—This is the same field that was defined in Chapter 4. For more information, see Section 4.2.1. It has been incorporated here for its relevance to material valuation.

VALUATION CATEGORY—The choice you make in this field will determine how different batches of the given material are valuated. For example, you may want to choose split valuation when a material can be both procured externally and produced in-house. This will allow each batch of the material to be valuated differently depending on the method of obtaining the material.

Conversely, if you choose to valuate all batches of a given material homogeneously, the system will only value the material as specified by the procurement type (either in-house or procured externally) that you've chosen in the MRP 2 screen of the material master. In this case, if the procurement type for a given material is procured externally (F), then any batch of the material produced in-house will be valuated as if it were procured externally, but a cost variance will be generated during financial settlement for that batch.

CURRENCY—This field is simply a display of the currency that you are working in. This currency is defined for you in the finance module.

CURRENT PERIOD—This field is another display-only field. It states the current fiscal period for financial settlement. Your fiscal year may very well differ from the calendar year, so the number of the period that you are in, as well as the year, may vary from the current numerical calendar month and year.

DIVISION—This field was previously defined in Chapter 5. For more information, see Section 5.2.1. This field was included here for reference to the division that the inventory value applies.

MATERIAL PRICE DETERMINATION: CONTROL—The setting that you make in this field is dependent upon which type of inventory valuation you are using, which you must define in the price control field in the next information set. You can either control inventory valuation by using the standard price or the moving average price in the PRICE CONTROL field. The choices that you make in the MATERIAL PRICE DETERMINATION CONTROL field will define in more detail how your price is controlled. It may not be necessary to maintain this field depending on your valuation method, but you have two choices to further your price control in material price determination control if you are maintaining material valuation in the material ledger:

▶ Transaction based (2)—If you have chosen to valuate your inventory on a moving average price "V", and you make the transaction-based (2) entry into the MATERIAL PRICE DETERMINATION CONTROL field, the moving average price is calculated and used to valuate inventory. If you have chosen standard price "S" in the PRICE CONTROL field, and you are using the transaction-based (2) control setting, your inventory will be valuated based on the standard price and the moving average price is calculated for reference only.

▶ Single / multi-level (3)—This setting is only used for the price control method of standard pricing "S". If you choose this setting in the MATERIAL PRICE DETERMINATION CONTROL field, your standard price will remain unchanged throughout all periods, but a periodic unit price will be calculated for each period once it is closed. Therefore, inventory will be valuated on the periodic unit price pertaining to each closed period and valuated on the standard price for all open periods.

MATERIAL LEDGER ACTIVATED AT MATERIAL LEVEL indicator—If this indicator is set to active, your materials are being valuated in a material ledger account. This is a setting that is made in SAP customizing. If you are valuating materials in the ledger account, you will have the ability to valuate materials in multiple ways and in multiple currencies. If this indicator is active, you will have the ability to make a material price determination control choice as defined above.

10.2.2 Current valuation

VALUATION CLASS—A valuation class can be assigned to a material to determine what general ledger accounts that valuated material is assigned to. You can specify in a valuation class whether materials of the same material type can to be settled to different general ledger accounts, or if materials of different material types can be settled to the same general ledger account. The valuation class can also be used to determine what goods movements will trigger an update in the general ledger account value.

The decision of how material is valuated is an actual accounting function. The valuation class is a means of directing inventory value to the appropriate general ledger account. The structure of your general ledger is defined by your financial controller or accountant and specific rules about valuation class assignments must be communicated to you if you are responsible for making this setting.

VALUATION CLASS FOR SALES ORDER STOCK—This field has the same function as the VALUATION CLASS field. However, this field allows you to maintain a separate valuation class for the same material in the case of sales order stock. Your accounting department may wish to settle inventory values of sales order stock to a separate general ledger account for segregated reporting purposes. If you are not using sales order stock, which is defined when you create the sales order for a given material, the standard valuation class is applied.

VALUATION CLASS FOR PROJECT STOCK—Just as VALUATION CLASS FOR SALES ORDER STOCK is used as an alternate valuation class, VALUATION CLASS FOR PROJECT STOCK can be used when settling to a defined project to allow for settlement to a general ledger account that differs from the standard valuation class rules.

PRICE CONTROL indicator—The choice you make in this field will determine whether you are going to use the standard price or the moving average price to valuate the given material's inventory.

As I mentioned in the introduction of this chapter, I recommend that you set the price control indicator to "S" for all finished and semi-finished goods and use "V" for all purchased items.

PRICE UNIT—This is the number of units that the standard or moving average price will apply to. For instance, if a dozen eggs costs $3.21, then the price unit should be 12.

MOVING PRICE—If you are using the price control for moving average price, that price will be displayed in this field. If the material ledger is activated for the material, and you are calculating a period unit price, that price is displayed in this field.

STANDARD PRICE—If you are using the price control for standard price, the standard price value is displayed in this field.

TOTAL STOCK—The total quantity of all valuated inventory for the given material is displayed here.

TOTAL VALUE—The total value of all valuated inventory for the given material is displayed here. This figure is the value that is posted to the balance sheet in financial accounting for the inventory value of the given material.

VALUATION BASED ON BATCH SPECIFIC UNIT OF MEASURE indicator—By activating this indicator you are telling the system that it is okay to valuate materials, by batch, in different units of measure, as you have defined as alternate units of measure.

FUTURE PRICE—If you enter a price in this field, it will become the valuated material price upon the future date specified in the valid from date field.

VALID FROM—This VALID FROM field differs from others that have been previously defined. This field applies specifically to future price.

PREVIOUS PRICE—This field displays the last active price, previous to the current price.

LAST PRICE CHANGE DATE—This field displays the last time the price was updated in the material master.

10.3 Accounting 2 screen

The ACCOUNTING 2 screen (see Figure 10.2) only has two information sets: DETERMINATION OF LOWEST VALUE and LIFO DATA. The fields within the DETERMINATION OF LOWEST VALUE information set are used to calculate taxes on a given material. The fields in the LIFO DATA information set are used to govern the valuation rules if you are in a last-in/first-out or first-in/first-out inventory environment.

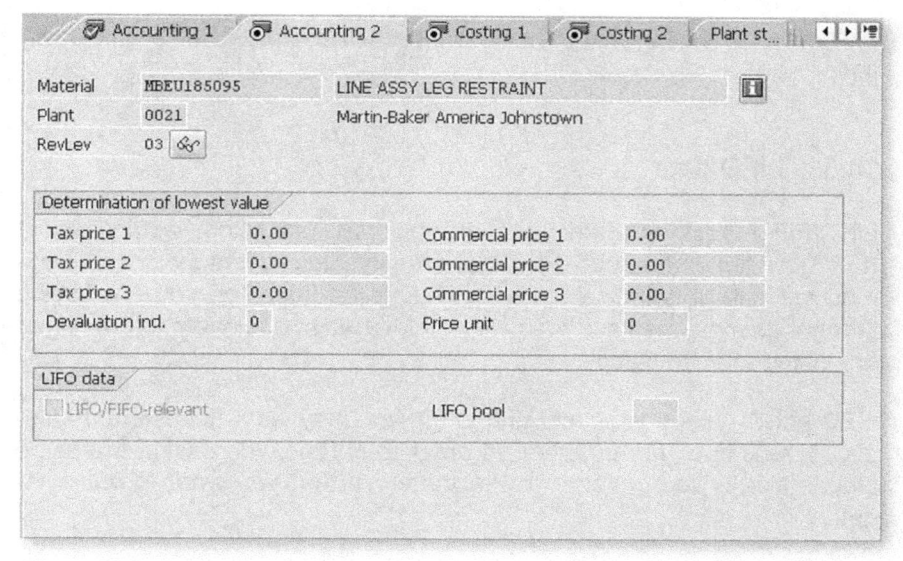

Figure 10.2: Accounting 2 screen

10.3.1 Determination of lowest value

The fields TAX PRICE 1 to TAX PRICE 3 and COMMERCIAL PRICE 1 to COMMERCIAL PRICE 3 are generic, despite their labels. They are information fields only and have no direct influence on any other system function. The fields were designed by SAP to use in inventory valuation. There are a number of functions in the MM inventory valuation which allow you to determine the lowest value for your inventory to adjust your balance sheet. These functions store intermediate results in these fields so that they can be read by subsequent functions. You can also enter values into these fields manually, or define a calculation variant in product costing to automatically enter values.

LOWEST VALUE: DEVALUATION indicator—If you are devaluing slow-moving or non-moving inventory, you can specify the number of years that the material is slow-moving or non-moving in this field. SAP will use this value, along with percentage rules established in SAP customizing, to calculate the material's value.

PRICE UNIT—This field is not the same as the price unit field that was previously defined. This field represents the price unit from the previous year. It is used to perform lowest value determinations and FIFO valuation.

10.3.2 LIFO data

LIFO/FIFO RELEVANT indicator—If you are practicing last-in/first-out (LIFO) or first-in/first-out (FIFO) accounting and inventory control, you must activate this indicator. By activating the indicator, you are saying that goods movements of the given material will be relevant to dates that are linked to each batch.

LIFO POOL—If you are practicing LIFO, you may want to valuate materials of the same type together. In order to do this, you assign the same alphanumeric pool number to the materials that you want to value together.

10.4 Costing 1 screen

The COSTING 1 screen (see Figure 10.3) contains two information sets: GENERAL DATA and QUANTITY STRUCTURE DATA. The fields within the general data information set are used to determine the costing type, overhead rate application, variance calculation rules, and other cost controlling features. The quantity structure data information set contains fields that govern how cost estimates are calculated when performing cost estimating with a quantity structure.

When performing costing in SAP, you are essentially entering the planned cost of producing or procuring a material into the system. You can either cost with or without a quantity structure. A quantity structure is created when you want to perform costing relevant to production quantities. It is generally useful to perform costing with a quantity structure, because you are using BOM and router data that will automatically calculate the cost in a costing run. The costing run will use the quantity structure that you define in the material master to make its calculation.

Alternatively, if you cost without a quantity structure, you must calculate the planned cost manually. This method is mostly used prior to full-scale production, when you do not have BOMs, routers, and production quantities established, but need to plan costs.

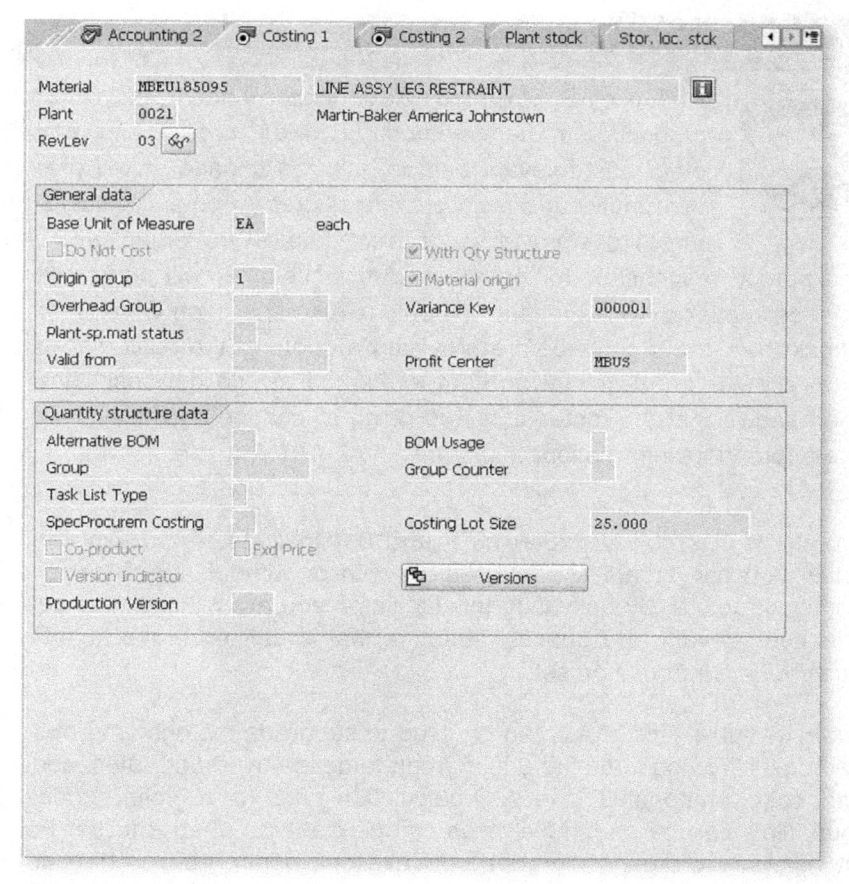

Figure 10.3: Costing 1 screen

10.4.1 General data

BASE UNIT OF MEASURE—This is the same field that was defined in Chapter 4. For more information, see Section 4.2.1. It has been incorporated here for its relevance to costing.

DO NOT COST indicator—By activating this indicator, you are preventing a material cost estimate from being created for this material. The material's cost estimate will also be prevented from inclusion in upper-level assemblies in which it is a component.

> ## Use the DO NOT COST indicator to prevent poor quotation.
>
>  I have often activated this indicator when I know that production routers/methods, BOMs, suppliers, or any other cost-relevant data is going to change. It will prevent individuals who provide quotes to potential customers from providing incorrect data. In my organization, the person responsible for quotation to the customer will perform a cost estimate on the material to be sold (SAP transaction CK11N) to check the current costs before providing a quote to the customer. If she receives an error that an item is marked as "do not cost," she then knows that the material cost is going to change and seeks out the appropriate information.

MATERIAL IS COSTED WITH QUANTITY STRUCTURE indicator—As I explained earlier, you can create a cost estimate with or without relevance to a quantity structure. By activating this indicator, you are making your cost estimates relevant to a quantity structure that is defined in the quantity structure data information set.

ORIGIN GROUP—This group can be used to subdivide material and overhead costs. You can use the origin group to define overhead rates, additional cost components, and WIP calculation rules for a given material group. This can be as simple or as complex as you need it to be. For instance, in my organization, we only use one origin group, which defines how overhead rates are applied to procured materials. Those materials that are produced in-house will already have their overhead rates applied in per our costing variant rules.

MATERIAL RELATED ORIGIN indicator—By setting this indicator to active, you are telling the system to update the cost element with reference to the material number. That is, the material number is recorded in the cost element alongside the costs. This is a critical piece of information when analyzing costs in the cost element. Otherwise, you will not have a frame of reference for where the cost came from. It is particularly useful if you are practicing settlement to a product cost collector, where you cannot easily identify a variance by work order because all variances related to the material are grouped together.

OVERHEAD GROUP—If you are interested in assigning different overhead rates to different materials within your plant, you can maintain separate overhead groups that can be applied to each material. You must first assign the appropriate overhead key to the overhead group in SAP customizing. You can then assign a costing sheet to your valuation variant or your production order that uses the overhead key contained in your overhead group.

VARIANCE KEY—The rules that you define in a variance key in SAP customizing will determine how variances from your target costs are calculated and reported. If you want to calculate variance, you must assign a key in this field.

Variance reporting and review is the most effective way to analyze your actual financial performance against planned costs in a large production environment. SAP has a robust variance calculator that provides that data for you. Otherwise, you would spend countless hours trying to collect and report the data. In my experience, it has been difficult to interpret the variance calculation, so be sure that you understand the output before making any decisions based on the variance report. It may be wise to invest in custom variance reporting if you are truly concerned with analyzing cost variances.

PLANT SPECIFIC MATERIAL STATUS—This field was previously defined in Chapter 6. For more information, see Section 6.2.1. The field is included here because those responsible for costing may have cause to implement a material restriction due to costing data.

VALID FROM—This field was also previously defined in Chapter 6. For more information, see Section 6.2.1.

PROFIT CENTER—This field was previously defined in Chapter 5. For more information, see Section 5.4.4.

10.4.2 Quantity structure data

ALTERNATIVE BOM—If you are not maintaining a production version that specifies your preferred BOM, you must define it here. The alternative BOM is the BOM of choice of a group of BOMs.

BOM USAGE—This field defines what the BOM is relevant to. You may maintain separate BOMs for the same material for different segments of the business, for instance, sales, production, engineering, universal, etc. As an example, if a BOM is not relevant to production it cannot be used to schedule planned orders. Again, you must define the BOM usage in this field if you have not already defined it by maintaining a production version.

KEY FOR TASK LIST GROUP—A task list group pertains to a group of routers. If you want to maintain different routers for the same material, you can use the task list group key in conjunction with the group counter to define which router should be used if you have not already maintained this data in a production version. The task list group key can be used to segregate routers for use by lot size quantity.

GROUP COUNTER—If not already maintained in a production version, you can define the router, within a group of routers, to be used when defined in conjunction with a task list group key. This is useful when you have several defined methods of production for the same material.

TASK LIST TYPE—If not already defined in a production version, you can define the type of task list being used. You have the following choices:

- ▶ Routings
- ▶ Reference operation sets
- ▶ Rate routings
- ▶ Reference rate routings
- ▶ Standard networks
- ▶ Rough-cut planning profiles

SPECIAL PROCUREMENT TYPE FOR COSTING—This field is useful if you want to use a different special procurement type for costing than you do for planning and production. If you do not define a special procurement type in this field, the system used the special procurement type in the MRP 2 screen.

COSTING LOT SIZE—This is the quantity of the material that your cost estimate will be based on. For example, if you normally produce widgets in lots of 50, it is best practice to set your costing lot size set to 50. This will give you the most accurate cost estimate, particularly in the way that setup time is amortized across the production lot.

If you are using scaled pricing in your purchasing info records, your costing lot size must fall within the quantity range of your purchasing info record in order to produce a cost estimate. Otherwise, the costing lot size quantity cannot identify with a price.

CO-PRODUCT indicator—This field was previously defined in Chapter 7. For more information, see section 7.3.1. It has been included here for its relevance to costing.

FIXED PRICE CO-PRODUCT indicator—If you have set the co-product indicator to active, you can set this indicator to active if you want to use a fixed price for your co-product that is not costed using a joint production process. Rather, you will define the cost of the co-product by installing a planned price in the material master or perform a cost estimate without a quantity structure. This can be useful when it is difficult to discern the cost of a co-product from the production method.

VERSION indicator—This field was previously defined in Chapter 7. For more information, see section 7.5.1. It has been included here for its relevance to costing.

PRODUCTION VERSION—A production version is where you control the BOM and router combination, along with other control parameters, that are used in production. You can maintain more than one production version for a material, but the calculation for a cost estimate must be based on only one cost estimate. This should really be the production version that is used most frequently.

PRODUCTION VERSION icon—This field was previously defined in Chapter 7. For more information, see section 7.5.1. It has been included here for its relevance to costing.

10.5 Costing 2 screen

The COSTING 2 screen (see Figure 10.4) contains three information sets: STANDARD COST ESTIMATE, PLANNED PRICES, and VALUATION DATA. The fields contained in the standard cost estimate information set are where you can view past, present, and future cost estimate information about your material. The planned prices information set is used to manually install prices for cost estimating when you are not performing cost estimates with a quantity structure. The fields within the valuation data information set are grouped together on this screen for your information due to their relevance to costing.

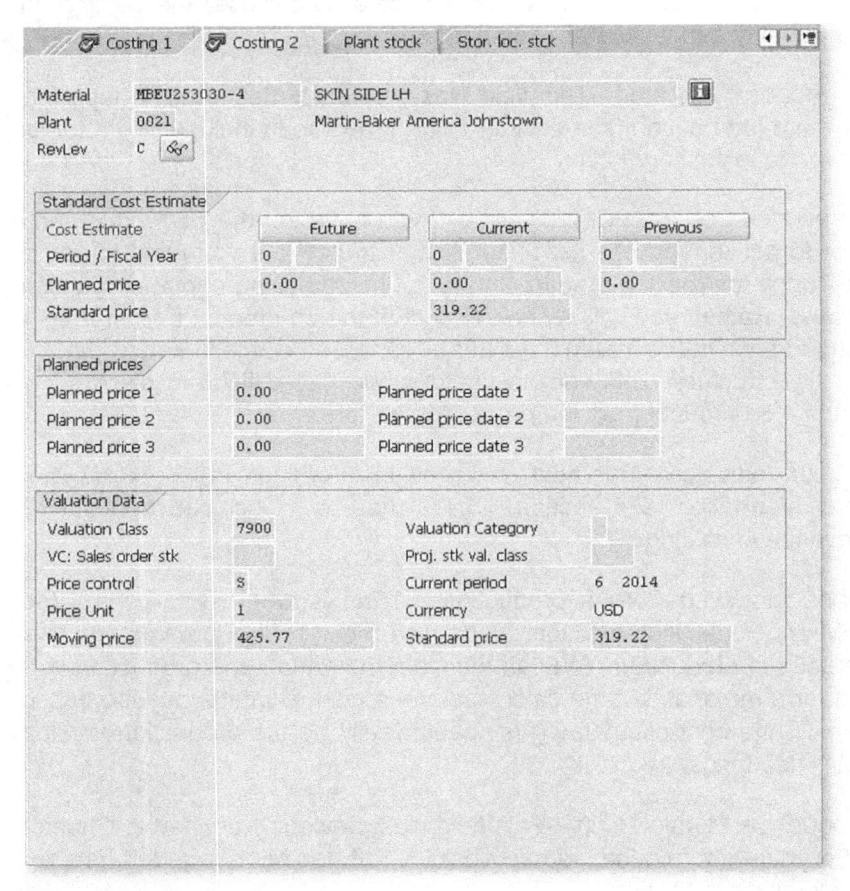

Figure 10.4: Costing 2 screen

10.5.1 Standard cost estimate

PERIOD / FISCAL YEAR—This is simply the period and fiscal year for which the cost estimate was, is, or will be valid.

PLANNED PRICE—There are three steps to creating a standard price. You must first create and save an error-free cost estimate (SAP transaction CK11N). If you perform an action called marking the cost estimate (SAP transaction CK24), that estimate becomes the planned price and will be stored in either the current or future cost estimate fields. Once a cost estimate is marked for a period, it cannot be changed. If you complete the third step, which is releasing the marked cost estimate (SAP transaction CK24), you will now have a standard price.

STANDARD PRICE—The standard price is the released cost estimate. It will be the basis of all financial calculations for goods movements. The standard price will remain unchanged until you choose to update it.

Update your standard price less frequently to keep costs low

The frequency in which you update your pricing will depend on your unique environment. However, if you are practicing standard pricing in a stable production environment where products have long lifecycles, I recommend updating your standard price no more than twice per year. This will help to establish a benchmark for variance analysis so that you can tell when prices are increasing in the next few periods. Otherwise, if you were to update the standard price every period, you would find that your variances are very low and meaningless, since you will be measuring the actual price paid against the most recent price update in your purchasing info records, which you can see in the example below (see Figure 10.5).

Period	Vendor price	STD price calculated semi-annually	Variance	STD price calculated every period	Variance
1	$10.00	$10.00	$0.00	$10.00	$0.00
2	$11.00	$10.00	$1.00	$11.00	$0.00
3	$30.00	$10.00	$20.00	$30.00	$0.00
4	$31.00	$10.00	$21.00	$31.00	$0.00
5	$9.00	$10.00	$1.00	$9.00	$0.00
6	$12.00	$10.00	$2.00	$12.00	$0.00

Figure 10.5: Standard price update frequency comparison

10.5.2 Planned prices

PLANNED PRICE—If you are not creating a cost estimate with a quantity structure, you may prefer to complete a manual cost estimate calculation. In that case, you can enter your calculated planned cost in this field. There are three planned price fields available so that you can restrict the validity period of the planned price and have it replaced by another.

PLANNED PRICE DATE—You can define the effective date of each planned price in this field.

10.5.3 Valuation data

All of the fields within the valuation data set were previously defined in this chapter under the ACCOUNTING 1 screen. For more information, see Section 10.2. These fields are included here as a reference to all relevant costing data.

10.6 Plant stock screen

The information sets contained in the PLANT STOCK screen (see Figure 10.6) are simply for detailed information about inventory values according to their status within the plant. This screen is useful for a quick view of your material's inventory level. However, much more robust inventory reporting features are available elsewhere.

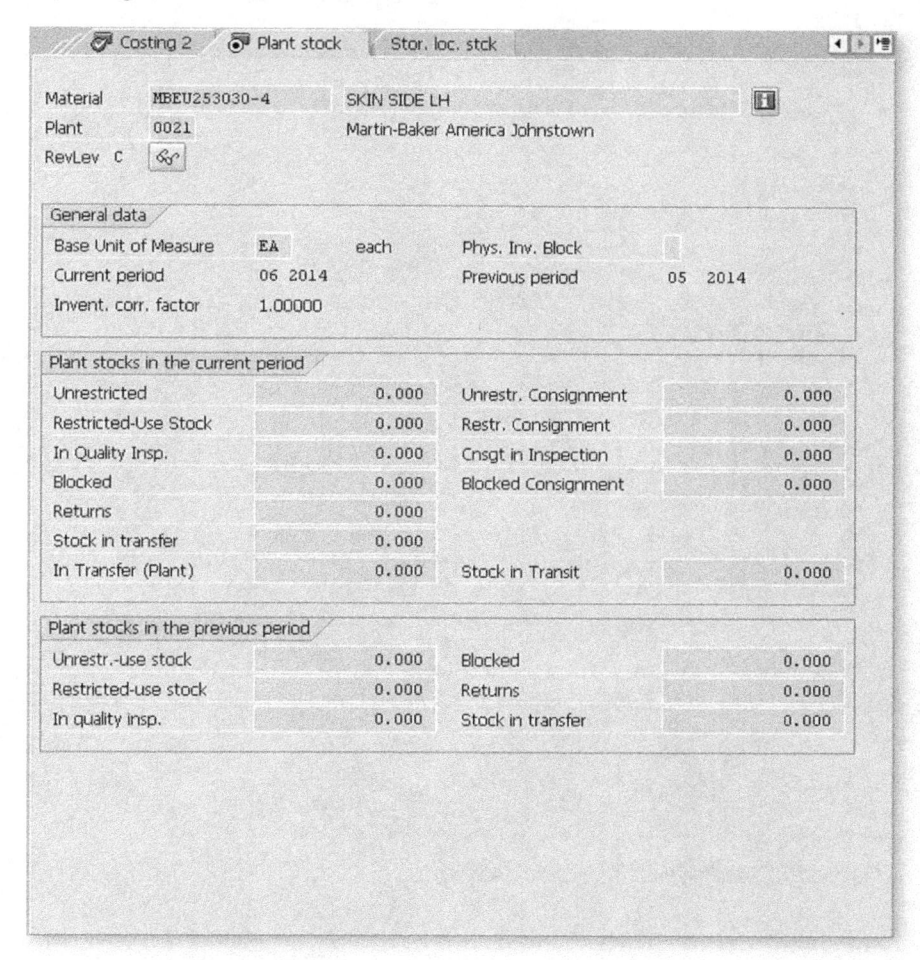

Figure 10.6: Plant stock screen

10.7 Storage location stock

Just as the PLANT STOCK screen is a quick reference for your material's inventory values, the STORAGE LOCATION STOCK screen (see Figure 10.7) reports the same data with the exception that the information provided is specific to only one storage location within the plant at a time.

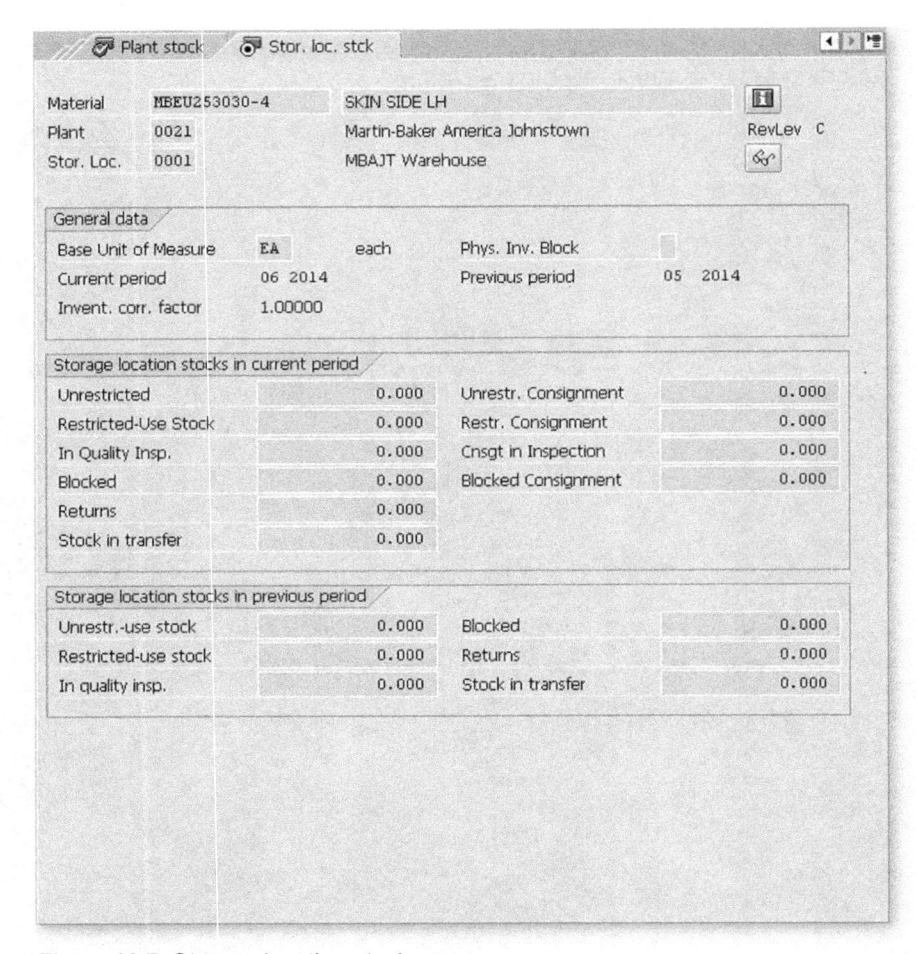

Figure 10.7: Storage location stock screen

10.8 Personal experience

It has been my experience with creating standard cost estimates that no other SAP-related task will give you a better picture of how production data is linked together in the system.

I recall our initial implementation of SAP, where all material masters were created in the system. We had an SAP financial consultant with us to guide the way. The consultant emphasized the importance of error-free cost estimates and that production and cost settlement would not get very far without them. Furthermore, we would not be able to judge our production performance without this baseline established.

Under the consultant's guidance, we began creating the cost estimates. My supervisor and I were tasked not only with creating the initial cost estimates, but also with resolving the resulting errors. At this point, neither I nor my supervisor knew what were about to embark on, a plant-wide rectification of all routers (and the many control elements within them), BOMs, production versions, and purchasing info records. As it turned out, we had missing links and parameters in just about every material in the plant. It was through the error elimination process that both he and I learned each contributing element to a successful cost estimate. Along the way, we learned a great deal about the production elements of SAP, because nearly every one of those elements is linked to the standard cost estimate in one way or another, and each of them has their own means of generating a costing error if they are missing or incorrect.

If you are tasked with or interested in learning how the SAP production system works, particularly in its relationship to financial controlling, I highly recommend that you attempt to learn the inner workings of creating standard cost estimates. If you can gain the permission to try different costing scenarios in a test client, you will gain a far better understanding of the system's overall structure.

11 Conclusion

In this chapter, I would like to recap the most important themes of the text in order to help you continue on your learning path of the SAP Material Master.

Well, I've had a lot of fun writing this text. It reminded me of all of the trials and tribulations that brought me and the team I work with to our current understanding of the material master. I hope that you have learned from this text, what I have learned from those experiences.

First and foremost, the impression I want to leave with you is that your work in the material master is never done. You will go through many different levels of understanding as time goes on if you are putting the work into it. I'm still going through them. Furthermore, once you do have a sound understanding, you should always be looking for better ways to use the material master to assist you in your continuous improvement efforts. As I have said before, in the SAP Material Master, there can be several different ways to achieve the same result. You must find the method that works for your unique circumstance in the most efficient way.

Secondly, I would like to reinforce that formally documenting what you do in the material master can go a long way. Not only the finely detailed documentation of your organization's procedures for the material master, but documentation of the testing you complete and the subsequent successes and failures of those tests. There are so many facets to the material master that you may find yourself repeating the same mistakes if you are not careful to capture your errors and their corrections.

Finally, I would like to leave you with my guiding principle that maintaining the material master is a team effort. Even if one group or individual is solely responsible for all material master maintenance, you will not be effective at all material master functions unless you are openly communicating with individuals from the respective functional groups. It is easy to get wrapped up in trying to control information out of fear or arrogance. You will only be able to grow intellectually and as a team if you set aside this hindrance to control information. Furthermore, if you are truly interested in continuous improvement and adding value to your organization, it behooves you to learn from others and form a bond of trust so that others may learn from you.

You have finished the book.

A The Author

Matt Johnson is a program manager at Martin-Baker America, Inc., a leading manufacturer of aircraft ejection seats and crashworthy helicopter seats. As one of the company's resident SAP super-users, he leads a continuous improvement team that strives for excellence in production efficiency and ERP innovation. Matt was educated at St. Francis University in organizational leadership, and maintains certifications in APICS Production and Inventory Management, APICS Supply Chain Management, as well as Lean Manufacturing. He has spent the past 14 years working in inventory management, production planning, sales and operations planning, continuous improvement, and program management, all in the SAP environment. Matt can be reached at *mjohnson122@verizon.net*.

B Index

D Disclaimer

This publication contains references to the products of SAP SE.

SAP, R/3, SAP NetWeaver, Duet, PartnerEdge, ByDesign, SAP BusinessObjects Explorer, StreamWork, and other SAP products and services mentioned herein as well as their respective logos are trademarks or registered trademarks of SAP SE in Germany and other countries.

Business Objects and the Business Objects logo, BusinessObjects, Crystal Reports, Crystal Decisions, Web Intelligence, Xcelsius, and other Business Objects products and services mentioned herein as well as their respective logos are trademarks or registered trademarks of Business Objects Software Ltd. Business Objects is an SAP company.

Sybase and Adaptive Server, iAnywhere, Sybase 365, SQL Anywhere, and other Sybase products and services mentioned herein as well as their respective logos are trademarks or registered trademarks of Sybase, Inc. Sybase is an SAP company.

SAP SE is neither the author nor the publisher of this publication and is not responsible for its content. SAP Group shall not be liable for errors or omissions with respect to the materials. The only warranties for SAP Group products and services are those that are set forth in the express warranty statements accompanying such products and services, if any. Nothing herein should be construed as constituting an additional warranty.

More Espresso Tutorials Books

Claudia Jost:

First Steps in the SAP® Purchasing Processes (MM)

- ▶ Compact manual for the SAP procurement processes
- ▶ Comprehensive example with numerous illustrations
- ▶ Master data, purchase requirements and goods receipt in context

http://5016.espresso-tutorials.com

Björn Weber:

First Steps in the SAP® Production Processes (PP)

- ▶ Compact manual for discrete production in SAP
- ▶ Comprehensive example with numerous illustrations
- ▶ Master data, resource planning and production orders in context

http://5027.espresso-tutorials.com

Sydnie McConnell & Martin Munzel:

First Steps in SAP® (2nd, extended edition)

- ▶ Learn how to navigate in SAP ERP
- ▶ Learn about transactions, organizational units, master data
- ▶ Watch instructional videos with simple, step-by-step examples
- ▶ Get an overview of SAP products and new development trends

http://5045.espresso-tutorials.com

Stephen Birchall:

Invoice Verification for SAP®

▶ Learn everything you need for invoice verification and its role in FI and MM

▶ Keep user input to a minimum and automate the process

▶ Discover best practices to configure and maximize the use of this function

http://5073.espresso-tutorials.com

Kevin Riddell, Rajen Iyver:

Practical Guide to SAP® GTS, Part 1: SPL Screening and Compliance Management

▶ Tips and tricks for leveraging SAP GTS to automate trade compliance

▶ Walk step by step through business processes

▶ Overview of regulatory requirements and compliance suggestions

▶ Review of Version 11.0 with screenshots

http://5100.espresso-tutorials.com

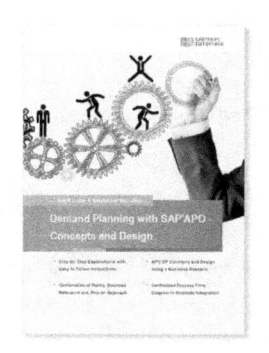

Avijt Dutta & Shreekant Shiralkar:

Demand Planning with SAP® APO—Concepts and Design

▶ Step-by-Step Explanations and Easy to Follow Instructions

▶ Combination of Theory, Business Relevance and 'How to' Approach

▶ APO DP Concepts and Design Explained using a Business Scenario

▶ Centralized Process Flow Diagram to Illustrate Integration

http://5105.espresso-tutorials.com

Avijt Dutta & Shreekant Shiralkar:

Demand Planning with SAP® APO—Execution

- ▶ Step-by-Step Explanations and Easy to Follow Instructions
- ▶ Combination of Theory, Business Relevance and 'How to' Approach
- ▶ APO DP Execution Explained using a Business Scenario
- ▶ Centralized Process Flow Diagram to Illustrate Integration

http://5106.espresso-tutorials.com

Kevin Riddell, Rajen Iyver:

Practical Guide to SAP® GTS, Part 2: Preference and Customs Management

- ▶ Best practices for leveraging SAP GTS for trade compliance
- ▶ Fundamentals of preference implementation and system set up
- ▶ How self-filing, broker models and free trade agreements can improve ROI
- ▶ Review of Version 11.0 with screenshots

http://5134.espresso-tutorials.com

Tobias Götz, Anette Götz:

Practical Guide to SAP® Transportation Management (2nd edition)

- ▶ Supported business processes
- ▶ Best practices
- ▶ Integration aspects and architecture
- ▶ Comparison and differentiation to similar SAP components

http://5082.espresso-tutorials.com

CPSIA information can be obtained
at www.ICGtesting.com
Printed in the USA
LVHW081441160521
687577LV00011B/630

9 781546 304173